# Agricultural Economics and Rural Land-use

## M. J. STABLER

*Lecturer in Economics*
*University of Reading*

*First published 1975 by*
THE MACMILLAN PRESS LTD
*London and Basingstoke*
*Associated companies in New York Dublin*
*Melbourne Johannesburg and Madras*

SBN 333 12700 5

*Printed in Great Britain by*
THE ANCHOR PRESS LTD
*Tiptree, Essex*

# Contents

# Preface and Acknowledgements

This is not a survey of agricultural economics; it is more concerned with the interaction between agriculture and other rural land-uses. As such it concentrates on the wider issues of agricultural activity in relation to advanced economies, where general economists, if not their agricultural counterparts, are increasingly concerned by the economic effect of such activities. A central feature of this concern is the impact of agricultural policy of farming and its associated effects on the rural environment.

Chapter 1 attempts to summarise the major aspects of what might be termed the 'traditional' approach to the economic analysis of agriculture, and acts as a foundation for an examination of the reasons for the form and objectives of intervention in the industry undertaken in Chapter 2. In Chapter 3 the effects on the agricultural sector of both the instruments and objectives are considered and in Chapter 4 the discussion is extended to assess the conflict between agricultural and other uses of land – urban areas, forestry, water-supply and recreation.

The references cited are virtually confined to the post-war period on a basis that they should be fairly typical, or represent a new approach, or include references to important studies elsewhere and be reasonably accessible.

I would like to acknowledge the support I have received from colleagues at Reading, for their helpful comments, particularly Paul Cheshire, who in numerous discussions helped me to formulate my ideas on the social costs of agriculture. I owe a special debt of gratitude to my wife, whose perception in making rude comments about the likely publication date of the book, whenever inquiries were made as to its progress, goaded me into completing it. I also wish to thank my mother, who helped to list and check the Bibliography; and Barbara Wall, who patiently typed and retyped the original drafts. Any errors or omissions which remain are entirely my own.

*December 1974*                                               M. J. S.

# 1 The Traditional Approach to the Economics of Agriculture

It is difficult to delineate the boundaries of agricultural economics, ranging as it does from the technical level of much farm-management work to psychology, sociology and planning. The problem is partially solved by accepting E. S. Mason's argument ('The Political Economy of Resource Use', in *Perspectives on Conservation*, ed. H. Jarrett; Resources for the Future, Johns Hopkins University Press, 1958) that the output and consumption of food products is sufficiently different from that of manufactured goods to justify it as an area of separate study, and may necessitate intervention by government agencies. According to Mason, the essential difference between manufacturing industries and agriculture is that the latter is characterised by inelasticity of supply and demand, which causes malfunctioning of the market mechanism, resulting in widespread repercussions on the operations of the industry and those engaged in it.[1]

Examination of the reasons for inelasticity in the supply of food products is, therefore, a convenient point at which to begin a survey of the economics of agriculture with the double aim of showing (1) how the industry affects other rural land-uses, and (2) what implications it has for society at large.

This chapter is largely concerned with the micro-economic analysis of agriculture and relies heavily on the existing texts

[1] Mason's discussion is much in the same vein as the concern which many agricultural economists in the United States show over the scope of their subject. They suffer recurring bouts of definitional fever, which makes for diverting reading. See the papers and proceedings of the American Economics Association published in the *American Journal of Agricultural Economics*. A typical example is an article by J. M. Buchanan, 'A Future for Agricultural Economics', *American Journal of Agricultural Economics*, vol. 51, no. 5 (Dec 1969.)

(See Bibliography, Section A – p. 85, which usually begin by examining the farm firm to illustrate the application of economic concepts. Attention is concentrated on the analysis of supply, and, in an attempt to keep the examination of studies on supply in agriculture fairly general, the following rather broad and arbitrary subdivisions have been adopted:

## 1   SUPPLY

(a)   Elasticity of supply.
(b)   The nature and use of resources.
(c)   Market structure.
(d)   The nature of uncertainty.

The order in which these subdivisions are given is not meant to suggest a logical development of the analysis except that the first as noted above, presents an opportunity to outline some fundamental propositions of supply in agriculture.

### (a)   Elasticity of supply

It is part of the conventional wisdom in agricultural economics that most of its problems are said to flow from inelastic supply combined with inelastic demand and, if there is a tendency for total supply to outrun total demand, then in a simple model price tends to fall. This normally has repercussions on farmers' income and future production plans; but the response by farmers is not always that expected from knowledge of entrepreneurial studies of other industries. Furthermore, it is advisable to look at the nature of agricultural products in seeking an explanation of supply elasticities. Thus two areas are of some significance: the nature of the product and farmers' reactions.

*The nature of the product.* Unlike most manufactured goods the *production period* in agriculture tends to be relatively long. Some animal products, such as poultry and pigs, can reach maturation, in terms of suitability for marketing, in weeks, but prime beef and dairy cattle may take several years. Arable crops have a minimum period of about six months, others may take one year

8

to mature, while tree crops require a number of decades before they are ready for the market. On the face of it such long periods would indicate that, once a decision to produce a particular commodity is initiated, there is very little a farmer can do if the price of that commodity changes. Hence a low price elasticity of supply is a continuing feature of agriculture. There is no doubt that the nature of the product does have this effect. However, two observations can be made. First, through technical change some shortening of the time periods may be possible and this might alleviate the problem. For example, new methods of rearing animals and new breeds may be adopted. Second, although the *aggregate* supply elasticity may be low, this is not always the case with *individual* products. If a farmer has specialised in one enterprise[1] (for example, the cotton farmer in the United States, or the arable farmer in East Anglia), then the response may indeed be slow. However, the mixed farmer may have more flexibility because he can make adjustments between enterprises within a relatively short period. The *seasonal* and *perishable* nature of much agricultural produce also tends to make for inelasticity, giving rise to gluts or shortages according to the timing of the production process.

The empirical evidence on the elasticity of supply is not particularly strong. The values derived naturally vary according to the time period taken, but nearly all aggregate supply elasticities are below 0·50. Most studies of aggregate supply functions have originated in the United States [141], [142], [147], [148]. M. Nerlove in a relatively early post-war study ('Estimates of the Elasticities of Supply of Selected Agricultural Commodities', *Journal of Farm Economics*, vol. 38, no. 2, May 1956), has suggested that it might be the method of measuring it which is at fault. His main criticism of aggregate supply studies is their predisposition to use changes in the acreage of crops as an index of supply changes. In any event, relating supply elasticities to the nature of the product alone is an oversimplification; factors attributable to capital and marketing are also applicable, as are those emanating from the farmer himself. In part, the work on a farmer's

[1] For the general economics reader the word 'enterprise' should be equated with 'product', as in the analysis of the theory of the firm.

9

response to price and supply changes suffers from the omission of such variables. Jones's study is an example of this kind of approach [146].

*Farmers' reactions.* Much of the research on supply is founded on the assumption that farmers base future production on the price prevailing in the current period. Keeping in mind the factors mentioned on p. 8, lagged supply functions combined with the current demand functions have been dubbed 'Cobweb Theorems' (see Fig. 1).

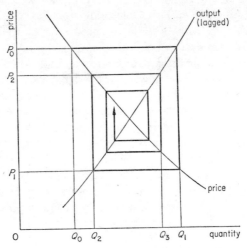

FIG. 1   Cobweb Theorem – diagrammatic representation

The demand curve (labelled 'price') relates current price to current production. The supply curve (labelled 'output lagged)') relates current supply to prices in the previous period. Thus, current output $(Q_1)$ indicates excess supply $(Q_0, Q_1)$ because output has been based on the prices which prevailed in the previous period $(P_0)$ when output was lower $(Q_0)$. Therefore, in the current period price falls $(P_1)$ and farmers plan to produce less $(Q_2)$ in the next period. This will result in a higher price $(P_2)$ in the next period, and this induces a higher output in the succeeding period $(Q_3)$, and so on.

As can be seen in Fig. 1, the price and output curves will

10

lead to an eventual equilibrium at the intersection of the curves as the oscillations are 'dampened' by the relatively less elastic supply curve. In a situation where a relatively more elastic supply curve were to be combined with the demand curve shown in Fig. 1 the oscillations would become greater. The former, described in detail, is an example of what is known as the 'converging' case; the latter is the 'diverging' case. A third case is one of 'continuous' oscillations where the 'cobweb' (shown as the thicker line) forms a rectangle or square. More complex examples of the simple cobweb have been constructed, but a more succinct way of illustrating them is through the use of equations.

This well-known analysis is said to be characteristic of all agricultural production, and two-dimensional models figure as such in many economic textbooks. However, a closer look at the studies listed in the Bibliography (Section A, p. 85) suggests that it is only characteristic of certain products and under certain conditions. Where the production period is relatively short, and where a full period is required to change the level of output, then a cycle emerges. In addition there are requirements that production should be carried on by many producers acting independently. Pig production tends to fluctuate in three-year cycles, while vegetable production follows a two-year cycle. Horticultural output is also subject to cycles because of reactions to prevailing prices. If, indeed, farmers react to high current prices by instituting plans to increase output, and the converse, then this has important implications for the economic analysis of supply and policy decisions on agriculture. For a fairly recent and detailed survey of cobweb models see F. V. Waugh, 'Cobweb Models', *Journal of Farm Economics*, vol. 46, no. 4 (Nov 1964), where the simple versions are shown to be part of more general lagged supply functions. These more sophisticated notions allow farmers to operate in terms of some expected price level which includes current and past prices in a distributed lag model [147]. A number of later models have included other variables as important determinants of supply: the conservative nature of many farmers, their age, management skills, expectations on policy and commitment to prescribed courses of action by past decisions on inputs. The weight given to these additional determinants may modify the simple conclusions flowing from recursive models. If

11

the farmer feels he is subjected to forces entirely outside his control a short-run 'do-nothing' policy may result. In the long run, discernible trends in the major variables are likely to induce a slow but positive response [146]. Farmers' slow reactions are inextricably bound up with their views of uncertainty on yields, but even here variations can lead to significant differences in planned and actual production. Quite small changes in supply, as a result of such factors when interrelated with inelastic demand, give rise to wide price variations, and these introduce a cyclical element into those commodities not ostensibly said to be so affected. Generally, in spite of these elements, the inclusion of more explanatory variables of farmers' likely reactions to price changes probably accounts for the lower values of aggregate supply elasticities as opposed to individual commodities.

(b)  *The nature and use of resources*

Factor demand and use is related to the price of the factor and the price of the product. Hence the economic approach to the use of resources in agriculture does not differ radically from that for any other productive activity. A more complex operational situation is likely to occur because farmers, unlike most manufacturing industries, tend to conduct multi-product activities.

The analysis of production at the individual farm level is the very essence of farm management and production economic studies, and the principles of farm-business activity are now firmly rooted in basic economic concepts which will be merely outlined here.

The fundamental decisions facing a farmer may be divided into those appertaining in the *short run* and those in the *long run* concerning the use of resources and level of output. In the *short run*, where he wishes to maximise output of a single product with at least one fixed resource, he is subject to the law of diminishing returns. In addition, the cost of resources will also determine the marginal cost of output which he needs to relate to the marginal revenue of the product. In situations where it is desired to attain a given level of output, the *combination of resources* becomes more important in order to minimise the cost of producing that given output, or in a more generalised situation, for several levels of output. Fig. 2 gives a diagrammatic

12

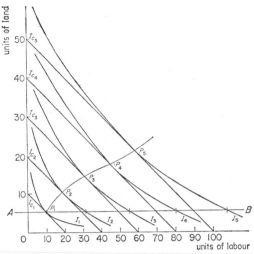

FIG. 2　The optimum use of resources – two-input case

$P_1$, etc., are points which trace out the output expansion path. $I_1$, etc., are isoquants, i.e. lines where the output produced by the two inputs is equal. $Ic$, etc., are isocost curves. In the figure the cost of each unit of labour is half that of land, i.e. twice the number of labour units can be purchased for a given outlay on land or labour.

representation of the attainment of the optimum use of resources in relation to their cost for a two-input (resource) case.

The points of intersection between the isoquant and isocost curves represent the least-cost combinations of land and labour. For example, if it is assumed that one unit of labour costs £5 and one unit of land £10, then for a given output of $P_1$, $I_1$ and $Ic_1$ indicate the least-cost combination of the two factors. If Fig. 2 had been drawn so that the spaces between the isoquants increased in distance from each other along the expansion path, working north-east from the origin, it would indicate decreasing returns to scale. This means that greater quantities of land and labour are required to obtain a given level of output. Actually, as shown, the expansion path indicates that, in relation to land, greater quantities of labour are being used as output is expanded. The line $AB$ gives the production function relating output to quantities of labour, i.e. for one variable output. In Fig. 2, diminishing returns to labour are shown because the distances

13

between the isoquants and their intersection with line *AB* are greater in moving from *A* to *B*.

If the more complex multi-product situation is examined the *combination of enterprises* is of crucial significance. Here the *marginal rate of transformation* between products needs to be known so that, ideally, where the *marginal rates of substitution* are equal the combination of products is determined. Thus a high degree of knowledge of product prices is required in order to make the optimum use of resources within each enterprise. In other words, adjustment in the use of factors is largely determined by changes in the relative prices of the different products. The *timing* of production is also important where the farmer can exercise some control as the state of the market will govern the selling price of his products.

Fig. 3 illustrates in a very simple form the foregoing passage by showing, for a two-product case, the best combination of products. The figure cannot offer an explanation on the timing of production.

It is assumed that the resources and their quantity are fixed.

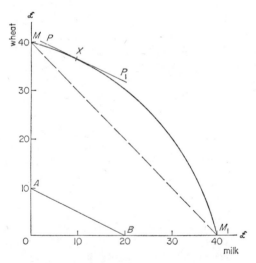

FIG. 3   Optimum product combination

*M–M₁* represents the marginal rate of transformation between wheat and milk. *P–P₁* is an isoprofit line.

14

The figure indicates the combination of milk and wheat which will be chosen. The fact that the continuous curve bows outwards from the origin means that total output is greater by combining products than specialising in one or the other, even though the products are competitive with each other. The broken line represents a case where the marginal rate of transformation is constant. This would suggest that, although milk production is competitive with wheat production, the expansion of milk by, say, one unit, would result in an equal reduction of one unit in wheat production. If the profit from wheat and milk were £10 and £20 per unit respectively (see the line drawn from £10 on the wheat axis to £20 on the milk axis, i.e. line $AB$) then the farmer would maximise profit by producing approximately $3\frac{1}{2}$ units of wheat and $1\frac{1}{2}$ units of milk. This is so because the iso-profit line $P-P_1$ which is parallel to the line $AB$ is tangential to the line $M-M_1$ at $X$.

The line $P-P_1$ could represent revenue in a situation where the profit for different levels of output for each product may not be determinable *a priori*.

In the *long run* the farmer still faces the complications which attend multi-product operations but he has a greater degree of freedom in substituting one factor for another. However, an additional dimension is introduced as changes in the *scale* of operations may determine the optimum use of resources and level of output.

Empirical evidence on economies of scale, in the United Kingdom at least, is somewhat scanty, despite theoretical arguments in its favour. A. H. Maunder has noted the effect on output of farm consolidation of a number of farms in England ('Farm Consolidation and Farm Output – A Note', *Farm Economist*, vol. 10, no. 7, 1964) where it was found that output fell. Farm consolidation refers to the use of land and fixed equipment and this may limit scale economies by offsetting those gained in the use of working capital and labour (see below, pp. 18, 24 on land and capital). In the *longer run* changes in *technique* and the rate of introduction of innovations adds yet another dimension. Metcalf [3a], in an excellent introductory text, summarises the major points on resource use and output which have been dealt with somewhat sketchily here.

15

If the variables discussed so far are incorporated into agricultural production functions the result is an extremely elementary representation of the farmer's operational situation. A host of additional and significant variables are important. For instance, the layout and structure of the farm unit, the quality of the resources, the constraints on their use – such as capital rationing, conservation of resources and the nature of uncertainty, as well as the less direct macro-economic and socio-political factors – are relevant. If the development of agricultural production economics is traced, from the very basic analysis of farm records between the two world wars to the adoption of more general economic methods in the 1950s and 1960s, it is apparent that it has not met the operational requirements of agriculture. This is due partly to the fact that the methods have not yet been refined sufficiently and partly because of the direction in which economics has led research.

Space does not permit the detailed examination of the development of the production function in general economics; Heathfield [144] surveys them at a theoretical level while Heady and Dillon [142] have made a contribution to their analysis in agriculture. Heady and Dillon outline the basic theory before giving extensive examples for different agricultural products. Unfortunately the work is not very useful because it is largely descriptive; little comment is offered on the functions included. Heady has been credited with changing the direction of agricultural production economics by emphasising economic rather than management concepts. More recent researchers have pursued the new course to such an extent that some economists feel that farm production functions have no operational significance whatsoever. G. L. Johnson, in a highly critical article ('Stress on Production Economics', *Australian Journal of Agricultural Economics*, vol. 7, no. 1, June 1963), accuses economists of being too simple, too descriptive, over-concerned with methodology, and neglecting the management aspects of production. He also feels that the functions only indicate what farmers ought to do under conditions of certainty and too little of what they actually do. These criticisms lead him to conclude that economists are excluding too many variables because of an obsession with a sterile positivism which is ill-conceived in the context of agriculture. He argues for

16

an approach which analyses production related to farmers' more immediate concern, such as labour and capital constraints through scarcity or financial problems. There is much truth in Johnson's argument, for the periodical literature abounds with articles applying and extending such techniques as linear-programming simulation, dynamic programming and game-theory analysis. In their crudest form the models rest on presuppositions of rationality and a high degree of knowledge on the part of the farmer. The research by Howard [145] illustrates the kind of approach to which Johnson objects, but work on game theory, such as that by Agrawal and Heady [102], Dillon [103] and Hazell [106], recognises the degree of imperfection and uncertainty in agriculture. However, the movement from the narrow range of production-function analysis to wider decision-making models still does not take the analysis far enough. The models do not indicate the required changes in the provision of fixed and working capital, land tenure, application of new techniques or the acquisition of new skills, nor do they include the influence of social, political and institutional factors. The references below to land (p. 18), capital (p. 24) and technical change (p. 30) respectively, contain some indication of these requirements. Variables such as those mentioned above are frequently omitted because of the use of secondary data which is incomplete, or is not available in the right form, or because it is not known how to incorporate them in the analysis. Indeed, in some instances the choice of variables is made almost arbitrarily, stemming from *a priori* reasoning as to which variables are likely to be significant, and to what extent, when making estimates of coefficients. This pursuit of a scientific base to agricultural economics, where the statistical shortcomings of the models are glossed over, lends a false air of precision to analyses. Where empirical work is carried out the validity and reliability is also sham, for predictions are very often based on small samples and may remain untested, or only be tested within extremely wide confidence limits.

Some confusion is caused by blurring the distinction between the production function, which springs from a technical relationship, and the supply function, which is an economic relationship taking account of both factor and product prices. Moreover,

17

supply functions can refer to the activity of one particular farm or business, a particular commodity, or at a generalised level, all agricultural production. Usually, however, supply function is a term applied to denote the production of a particular commodity at an aggregate level. As such it suffers the complications well known as the aggregation problem. Production and supply functions represent the demand for all farm resources; equally important are the components of the functions. Much work of an empirical nature has been carried out on hypotheses relating to the determinants of demand for individual resources and their characteristics [139], [140], [143], [149], [150]. Examination of work in this field is essential and some discussion of it follows.

The approach adopted is to consider the most important areas of interest within the accepted classification of resources except that enterprise is linked with labour under Human Resources (p. 33) because of the virtual embodiment of one in the other in agriculture.

The order in which each resource is considered is first land; second, capital; and then human resources.

*Land.* Land as a factor can be considered in two ways. The first is at the individual farm production level where from a financial, and to an extent from a farm management viewpoint, land is just another form of capital. This view is based on the supposition that the inputs, in the form of fertilisers, livestock and machinery, alone determine the yield from the land.[1] At worst, this implies that farm location, size, layout and forms of tenure are irrelevant or, at best, included only as a constraint. Yet aspects such as these have continued to be examined as determinants of farm efficiency and development and thus merit serious attention. The second way in which land ought to be considered is in the wider context in which agriculture operates. In both the United States and Europe there has been much concern over low incomes in agriculture, which has encouraged research into the control of the agricultural use of land. Of more recent origin has

[1] In the 1950s a number of writers argued that land as a factor had declined in importance – see as an example T. W. Schultz, *Economic Journal*, vol. 61, no. 244 (Dec 1951) and *The Economic Organisation of Agriculture* (McGraw-Hill, 1953) ch. 8, pp. 125–46.

been the change of use of rural land. Loss of land to urban use seems to be a particularly British preoccupation, but pressure for the alternative uses of land, other than for purely agricultural activity, now stems from the increased demand for resources such as minerals, timber, water and recreational use. This raises questions regarding the multiple use of rural land. It is largely the first aspect of land, as a factor, which is discussed here. Examination of the much wider issues are deferred until later in the study.

The major areas of interest related to land are: farm size, structure, layout and location; forms of tenure, land values and land-use. The incorporation of land into the resource demand function and its characteristic in terms of diminishing marginal productivity and diminishing marginal rate of substitution is part of very basic agricultural production economics, an outline of which was given in general terms above and so will not be pursued further.

*Farm size, structure, layout and location.* It is argued that farm size, structure, layout and location should be incorporated in agricultural economics because they are important determinants of economic efficiency. The arguments are related to the indivisibilities associated with certain factors, notably entrepreneurial capacity, labour and machinery on the one hand, and specialisation on the other [7], [11]. However, the optimum size of a farm is a function of its main enterprises and the degree of specialisation possible : arable farming is susceptible to the economics of scale, dairy farming is not so [4]. But specialisation has its own limitations since monoculture can eventually lead to the exhaustion of the productive quality of the soil and incidence of plant pests, and larger numbers of livestock increase the risk of disease (see Chapter 4). Despite these limitations, inspection of statistics of farm size suggests that in most countries the scale of operation is too small. For example, the average size of farms in the United Kingdom is less than 100 acres, while European farms are even smaller.

Contrary to popular belief, of over 3 million agricultural holdings in the United States, well over 60 per cent are less than 200 acres in area (see R. F. Boxley, 'Farm Size and the Distribution of Farm Numbers', *Agricultural Economics Research*, vol. 23, no. 4, Oct 1971). Reference to statistics over time, both in the United States and United Kingdom, shows the average size of farms is tending to increase, albeit slowly.

Other factors do influence this trend; indeed, they are apt to offset the amalgamation of farms (see the references to human resources and uncertainty, pp. 33, 42). A distinction between size of farm and holdings should also be made. The total acreage under the control of one farmer may be quite large but the fragmentation of the holdings or parcels of land may be extensive. It is fragmentation which is a bar to increasing the efficiency of agriculture; this is particularly so in Europe where it is related to forms of tenure and is hindering long-term structural change.

Although there is much evidence supporting the claim that the *size* of farms should be larger, the determination of the *optimum size* for the reasons already given is far from being ascertained. One reason for this is that theoretical models are often inadequately specified, but this is understandable in a dynamic situation if the fluctuation in production, market changes and technical improvements are appreciated. Another reason is that although there is a wealth of theoretical postulations the empirical studies, necessary to test any hypotheses, are not common [9].

The structure of a farm refers to the proportion of each resource used. Generally the quantity of land in relation to other resources, i.e. its combination with other resources, is taken as an indication of farm structure. The layout as well as the structure is alleged to be an important determinant of efficiency, but for this there is very little supportive evidence. This is again related to the dearth of empirical studies, of which those by Maunder are an exception. In the study to which reference has already been made on p. 15, Maunder found no clear evidence that consolidation, which includes altering the layout of farms, has increased output and, by implication, efficiency.[1] His findings, which drew on the work of others on farm amalgamation where

[1] See also A. H. Maunder, 'Some Consequences of Farm Amalgamation', *Westminster Bank Review* (Nov 1966).

an increase in the number of acres occurred, were that marginal product also increased, particularly on larger farms. This offers evidence in favour of large-scale farming; Maunder argues that the fixed factors are combined better with variable factors. He concludes, however, that the improvement in marginal product will merely lead to increased land values and prices, so that farming net income does not necessarily increase.

Dixey and Maunder [7], in a study of dairy farms in the United Kingdom, in which they estimated the likely effect of farm size and layout on efficiency, found that both the amalgamation of farms and changes in their layout would improve efficiency. They do not press the claims too strongly, for the study was a small one and hedged about with many qualifications. A study by M. B. Jawetz (*Farm Size, Farming Intensity and the Input–Output Relationship of some Welsh and West of England Farms*, University College of Wales, Aberystwyth, 1957) conflicts with their results. He found that the expected profit on small farms was as good as on larger ones.

Following the work of J. M. von Thünen (*The Isolated State*, trans. C. M. Wartenberg, Pergamon, 1966) many have studied the relationship between distance from the market, transport costs and optimum land-use (J. W. Birch, 'Rural Land Use and Location Theory: a review', *Economic Geography*, vol. 39, 1963). These variables determine the rent which agricultural land will command and the farm enterprises which will be undertaken in a spatial sense. For example, von Thünen argued that high-value bulky and weighty farm products, such as vegetables, would be grown near the market, while cattle would be reared at greater distances from the market. He concluded that rent would decline with distance from the market, and this has largely been borne out by more recent studies. However, technical change which has led to changes in production processing, transport and marketing, has weakened von Thünen's argument. It is only at a theoretical and individual farm level that the distance from the farm to its fields exercises an influence on land-use (see a survey by M. Chisholm, *Rural Settlement and Land Use*, Hutchinson, 1962).

*Form of tenure.* As an aspect of land as a resource the form of

21

tenure is a neglected area of study in agricultural economics relating to industrial nations. Earlier studies were largely concerned with the form of tenancy as a determinant of intensity of utilisation and efficiency [18]. One persistent argument is that various forms of share-tenancy – share cropping is an example – militate against increasing production. The basic explanation is that the tenant will produce to the point where his marginal revenue is twice his marginal costs, as a half-share of his profits will be paid to the landlord. Empirical studies, however, do not bear out the theoretical point. A recent study by Cheung [3] has attempted to prove that even on theoretical grounds share-tenancy can lead to the efficient use of resources. Another aspect of tenure form is whether the relative security of tenure has an effect on efficiency. If the tenant has security he is likely to undertake long-term investment to improve the farm business, but this depends on the respective contributions of capital by landlord and tenant [2], [12], and arrangements for reviewing rents. Complete security can be an inhibiting factor in farm values, as can be ascertained by studying the sale prices of farms in vacant possession, and those with sitting tenants, in the United Kingdom between 1945 and 1958 when rents were controlled. Farms with sitting tenants sold at lower prices than those with vacant possession. This is undoubtedly related to the control which the purchaser has over the rent charged, the possible non-economic motives for purchasing farms, and their availability. H. A Thomas ('Aspects of the Economics of Land Ownership', *Journal of Agricultural Economics*, vol. 18, no. 2, May 1967) has suggested that, for farms of comparable size, owner-occupiers appear to undertake more investment in fixed equipment than tenants; this is confirmed in the studies by Black [2] and Maunder [12]. However, Thomas also found that owner-occupiers tend to enjoy lower net incomes than tenants. This is related to the taxation commitments which might face the owner-occupier. All writers emphasise the complications of studying investment in agriculture. They also agree that it is not a well-studied area in agricultural economics and that there is a need to ascertain the capital requirements for different types of farms and the degree to which capital constraint affects farming efficiency.

22

Although the owner-occupier should have the incentive to farm efficiently, in periods of rapidly rising land prices, both in terms of purchase and opportunity cost, the owner may face a severe capital constraint. In the United Kingdom, up to the late 1960s, owner-occupiers accounted for about 50 per cent of farm holdings. There are signs now that the trend towards owner-occupation is being reversed and evidence suggests that this is due to problems related to capital availability. R. Gibbs and A. Harrison, *Land Ownership by Public and Semi-public Bodies in Great Britain* (University of Reading, 1974), estimated that 8 per cent of agricultural land is owned by corporate landowners and that this percentage is increasing. Harrison's continuing study of investment in agriculture (for example, *The Farms of Buckinghamshire*, Miscellaneous Studies, no. 40, University of Reading, 1966), underlines the problems facing farmers in financing changes in production patterns, and undertaking expansion. He notes the relatively minor role that landlords play in the investment in fixed equipment of an essential nature and the overwhelming role of owner-occupation in terms of the proportion of total investment in agriculture.

Studies on the effect of different forms of tenure therefore seem inconclusive [10]. This is partly because of the lack of data which might show significant differences and partly because of the technical difficulties in measuring the effect. It is probably true to conclude that in industrial nations different forms of tenure are not significant in themselves; it is the indirect effect that tenure has on the provision of capital which is more significant. To date, studies taking this line of approach are comparatively rare [20].

*Land values.* The majority of work on land values is orientated towards describing and explaining fluctuations in land prices and rents over time. [14], [15]. At a theoretical level the exercise can be justified as an attempt to establish the return to land, for two reasons. First, as a means of assessing the productivity of land as a measure of the economic efficiency of agriculture, and, second, it can reveal the opportunity cost of the agricultural use of land. Actual land-use studies in agriculture have been undertaken at two levels. There are the intra land-use studies, which are very largely within basic farm management studies, concerning the optimum mix of enterprises; and there are inter land-use studies. Calculation from farm records of actual income per acre is possible, and information on rents and prices is readily available. From these in the United Kingdom, estimates have been made of the return to land, often proving negative, particularly if the farm is relatively small [139]. However, in attempts to measure the opportunity cost of land having established land values, very little predictive use is made of the results, and it can be argued that little use *can* be made of them. The reasons lie in the determinants of agricultural land values from outside agriculture, ranging from the tax structure, political, planning and financial institutions, the rate of urbanisation, the interest rate, the level of economic activity and inflation at a general level, to location, fertility, market conditions and technical change at a particular level. Work done in the United Kingdom by Ward [112] and Wibberley [113] in the late 1950s, in connection with the conservation of land, highlighted some of the difficulties in arriving at 'true' returns to land. The Ward and Wibberley studies previewed what is now a pressing need – the evaluation of the true return to land in agriculture in order to facilitate decisions regarding rural land-use. This work is surveyed in more detail in Chapter 4 where the relationship between agriculture and other land-uses is examined.

*Capital.* The use of the word 'capital' causes some definitional problems. In the United Kingdom it is used in a legal sense to distinguish between the landlord's and tenant's responsibilities (roughly equated to fixed and working capital respectively), and as such it includes land. These problems are only partially resolved in an analytical context in general economics, quite apart from application to agriculture, as identification of the contribution by capital to output is complicated by such factors as technical innovation, relative output and factor prices, capital consumption and changes in scale. However, although a substantial part of work on agricultural production functions is concerned with capital as a variable, other major areas of interest outside that rather specialised field do not attempt to make a precise distinction, despite a need for doing so. Work on agricultural economics on capital centres on :

investment in capital,
the rate of return on capital,
technical change and the adoption of innovations and
capital credit.

With the exception of the last, studies have drawn heavily on work originating in general economic analysis, therefore reworking the whole of the ground is not necessary.[1] The recent work on the four areas given is thus examined within the context of agriculture only.

*Investment in capital.* The principle capital inputs in agriculture are buildings, tractors, machinery, seed, feed, livestock and fertilisers. Studies of investment in these inputs have been undertaken at a particular level in response to questions on decision-making in agriculture and, at the more general level, on the relationship between the agricultural sector and the rest of the economy.

At the particular level indentification of the determinants of demand for inputs and specification of the function have been pursued as part of agricultural supply functions. At the more general level agricultural expansion programmes and agriculture's contribution to economic growth have generated interest in the rate of investment leading off into questions related to the rate of return on capital, its opportunity cost, productivity and the importance of the agricultural industry in the economy [17].

Investment functions have been constructed which tend to follow in form those in general economic analysis, and thus the problems are largely the same [139]. The major difficulties are measuring the flow of capital services and the motivation of the investor. The derivation of dynamic rather than static functions is seen as an essential development of the models and involves the making of assumptions about the rate of investment to replace the existing stock of capital or to increase it in response to influences on the farmer. For example, it is assumed that increases in product prices leading to higher farm income will induce investment.

However, as in other industrial sectors, the investment plan

[1] Attention is drawn to the Bibliography (Secion B, p. 85) for standard works on the economic analysis of resources.

and its execution are not completed within a specified time period so lags are incorporated into the function. Thus most work on agricultural investment functions appears to result in the familiar stock adjustment models with the inclusion of distributed lags to simulate a dynamic situation. The principal determinants of investment are seen as the product price, lagged gross income, the farmer's ability to pay (which may depend on past income, and also on his ability to borrow), his expectations on prices and income, his age and level of education, attitudes to risk and uncertainty and the form of tenure, the rate of technical change, the interest rate as well as government policy directly or indirectly related to agriculture. It is readily apparent that including expectations and attitudes necessitates some heroic assumptions and impairs the efficiency of the investment function as an explanatory tool. A recent development has been the use of simulation models of investment where the heterogeneity of investment in agriculture is broken down into steps to consider alternative plans in order to effect specification of a general model [6]. Nevertheless, the evidence flowing from rather crude models of investment supports more rudimentary methods which show that investment in agriculture has taken a form, in industrial nations, which leads to the substitution of capital for labour. The reasons are not hard to find. Government support for agriculture by maintaining product prices and by giving direct production grants has raised farm incomes, which has encouraged not only investment in agriculture but resulted in the movement of factor prices in favour of capital. Both increased investment in agriculture and the substitution of capital for labour have encouraged study of the role of capital in the sector. Some studies have been concerned to relate the experience in industrial nations to economic development in less advanced economies, while others have sought to explain effects within the economy of the country examined.[1] Much work has also been highly critical of policies which have resulted in the expansion of the agricultural sector. Some scrutiny of this work is called for at this point whereas detailed examination of government policies and the wider

[1] Work on agricultural development and agriculture's contribution to growth is not pursued very far in this survey.

implications of an expanding agriculture are taken up again in Chapters 3 and 4.

*The rate of return on capital.* Research on capital in agriculture connected with its opportunity cost, productivity and the contribution of the agricultural sector to the economy must entail the calculation of the rate of return on capital. The difficulties of defining and distinguishing capital have already been outlined and they are an important aspect of methodologically orientated studies on capital. Peters [16] sparked off a controversy on Incremental Capital Output Ratios (I.C.O.R.s) in United Kingdom agriculture which became diverted towards issues concerning identification of gross and net investment. Work by Cocks [5] on Discounted Cash Flow (D.C.F.) techniques foreshadowed more recent disscussion of methods of capital appraisal which agricultural economists have taken up from cost–benefit analysis. The new controversy is the relevance of internal rate of return and net present value as appropriate methods for determining the level of investment. Agricultural economists have been rather slow in debating capital appraisal techniques which have been well aired in economic literature. The relevance of considering capital appraisal techniques here is that problems related to discounting arise where agriculture is compared with forestry and where the returns on agriculture are capitalised, as in the studies by Ward and Wibberley [112], [113].

Notwithstanding the problems associated with calculating the rate of return, to date studies of farm incomes have indicated that return on capital invested in agriculture is very low on all except the largest farms. Estimates of the return on capital in agriculture are complicated by the close relationship between land and fixed equipment and the system of subsidies, grants and taxation. C. I. C. Bosanquet ('Investment in Agriculture', *Journal of Agricultural Economics*, vol. 19, no. 1, Jan 1968) has used M.A.F.F. figures on net farm income to calculate the landlord's and tenant's return on capital invested, for different sizes and types of farm. The studies of land-use [122], [127], and the contributions by Hampson [123] and James [124] on the return to forestry, include estimates on the return to agriculture. The maximum return is given at about 10 per cent, and, at the other

27

end of the scale, the return is often negative. The work on investment, discussed above in the context of tenure, also implies that the return on capital is low, particulary where the farm is owner-occupied since net farm income is also very low.

The fact that the return in agriculture compares unfavourably with that in industry raises questions on the level of investment, the efficiency of capital so employed and its opportunity cost.

Statistics on productivity for O.E.C.D. countries [1] suggest that it has increased rather slowly since the Second World War. In the United Kingdom studies of productivity measurement [8], [13] indicated that up to 1968 output grew at about $1\frac{1}{2}$ per cent per annum, which was somewhat slower than in other industrial sectors. This has been achieved by large increases in the capital inputs in relation to land and labour so that productivity for labour has appeared to be very high. In the case of land, the rate of increase in productivity has not been so high because diminishing returns related to, for example, artificial fertilisers utilised, appear to have set in earlier. The importance of studying productivity in agriculture is related to that obtained in other sectors. In a relatively free-market situation, if the productivity of an input is higher in one sector than another then the price mechanism will ensure the transfer of resources. Even if the productivity of capital in agriculture was higher than in manufacturing industry, this would not necessarily suggest that resources should flow into agriculture. Two qualifications are important: first, productivity is basically a physical measurement, and increased output needs to be converted into value terms. This is determined by the demand for agricultural products, which is relatively inelastic. Second, government support for agriculture has interfered in the normal market mechanism to such an extent that resource prices do not reflect their true value in a particular use quite apart from the state of competition in the market. Thus it is also difficult to measure the efficiency of use of capital in agriculture and its true opportunity cost. Using existing measures of the productivity of capital and its rate of return and an indication of efficiency and opportunity cost respectively, it is clear that in most countries both are lower in agricultural than in other sectors of the economy. This suggests

28

that the agricultural sector is larger than it would otherwise be. One rider should be added, however; a sector can be larger than it should ultimately be if the process of movement of resources out of it is rather slow because of factors affecting the mobility of resources. Another factor may well be that based on the infant industry argument, i.e. that agriculture can enjoy economies of scale in the future if resources are retained in it until such time as it becomes economically viable.

In agriculture there is evidence that human resources are the least mobile; this is borne out by the relatively low returns which farmers are willing to accept. One further problem in being precise about the relative efficiency of agriculture has been the lack of data in a suitable form for analysis.

Because of the tendency for capital resources to be artificially retained in agriculture, work on productivity and calculation of rates of return has engaged the interest of economists. Much more recently it has been the general economist rather than the agricultural economist who has cast a sceptical eye on the use of resources in agriculture. For example, highly critical views have been expressed by McCrone [83], and, on a perhaps more fundamental level, the environmental economists represented by the work of Kneese *et. al.* [120]. Those who argue in favour of increasing the capital input of agriculture to a level higher than market trends would suggest, do so on two grounds. First, the contribution of agriculture to economic growth and second, on social or political grounds. For example, in the United Kingdom there are arguments in favour of maintaining farming income on social grounds, and to expand agricultural production, because of its import-saving role, on political grounds. Questions such as these are only answerable if, again, estimates are made of efficiency and the opportunity cost of the resources in agriculture. (The reason for mentioning agriculture's role in the economy, within this section, is that agricultural policies tend to emphasise capital intensive methods.)

In industrial economies the conflict on agriculture's role in contributing to economic growth has been conducted on two fronts. First, on how capital injection can lead to the release of labour for use in other sectors, where there are labour shortages; and second, on the efficiency of agriculture *vis-à-vis* other sectors.

A good example of comparisons between agriculture and other industrial sectors within a country and agriculture in one country compared with agriculture in another, is the study carried out by Sharp and Capstick [19] on the place of agriculture in the economy. It examined the import-saving role, the volume of output and competitive position of agriculture. Whether it is economically sound to maintain agriculture obviously depends on the comparative advantage it enjoys rather than its efficiency in an absolute sense. Sharp and Capstick's study concludes that agriculture's contribution is uncertain, if not negative, for import-saving. The evidence they gave suggested that the cost of home-produced importable foodstuffs was higher than the cost of imported food, while evidence on agriculture's contribution to the balance of payments was inconclusive. However, examination of government-induced investment of capital inputs in agriculture moves the survey from analysis of resources into questions of policy. Therefore, further discussion is curtailed until the theme is taken up again in Chapter 3, devoted to the economic effects of policy.

*Technical change and the adoption of innovations.* The analysis of technical change constitutes a component in the study of production functions and it has proved to be a difficult variable to handle. The pioneers in this field of study were K. J. Arrow *et al.*, who, in 'Capital Labour Substitution and Economic Efficiency', *Review of Economics and Statistics*, vol. 43, no. 3, (1961), attempted to embody technical change into different forms of the production function (see also K. J. Arrow, 'Notes on Production and Transmission of Technical Change', *American Economic Review*, vol. 59, no 2, and Heathfield [144]). The major problem in the incorporation of technical change has been identifying changes in the quality of the capital input and its effect on other inputs. For example, combine-harvesters have become larger and more powerful and thus shortened the harvesting process. This has also improved labour productivity and thus has conceivably reduced costs of both capital and labour inputs. G. F. Donaldson and J. P. McInerney ('Combine Capacity, Harvest Uncertainty', *Farm Economist*, vol. 11, no. 4, 1967) argue that because of uncertainties relating to weather and

30

harvest conditions most farmers 'over-invest' in combines, i.e. have spare capacity.

A further complication is that there is not necessarily a change of technique as far as the farmer is concerned: the farm production function remains the same but technical change in, say, the combine industry, reduces the price of a combine leading to a substitution effect in favour of the cheaper input. Early production functions yielded results with high residuals, attributable to technical change [152], [157]. Better specification of the functions has led to a reduction in these residual values by including variables increasing the explanatory power of the inputs. Some such variables are changes in machinery size and power, labour skill, farm layout, etc. However, changing specifications over time is merely another way of embodying technical change in the functions. The importance of identifying technical change lies in the precision which can be attained in production and supply functions in accounting for change and making estimations. This has implications for both decision-making by the individual farmer and the government. There is, however, an aspect of technical change which has wider implications for agricultural growth and development: this is the rate at which innovations are adopted. Although the problems of analysing technical change are formidable, the inclusion of the rate of adoption increases them. The analysis of what is called the 'diffusion of innovations' studies the time period between the invention of the technique and its application. Innovations have two effects: they reduce costs and change the nature of the process. For example, a new type of milk parlour not only reduces costs, but also changes the technique of milking.

The study of the adoption process comes more properly in the province of rural sociology [155] than economics, and as a result is viewed by some economists with acute suspicion. A comprehensive review article by G. E. Jones [154] summarises the important areas of interest in the study of innovation. The relevant aspects are the source of knowledge and characteristics of the new technique, the attributes of the farmer, the rate at which it is adopted, the spatial diffusion and the ultimate level of utilisation [151], [153], [156]. Some important characteristics of the technique are its price and the effect on the level of costs.

Farmers' attributes include age, education, income and nature and size of enterprise.

The implications of 'socio-economic' studies are greater for predominantly under-capitalised economies. The example of the 'Green Revolution' highlights the consequences of ill-founded applications of techniques by outside agencies of new strains of grain in Asia. The social, economic and technical attributes of farmers in the recipient countries were not equal to the quality of the new input, thus leading to its partial failure as an improved technique. Agricultural economists should be held equally responsible with scientists for this failure in ignoring or underestimating important attributes. The role of the sociologist has been underrated in the applied field of economics, and yet there is an extensive literature in sociology which has examined the social prerequisites for economic change to be effective.[1] Ruth Gasson [41] offers some observations on the importance of sociology in agricultural economics with particular reference to farmers' motives and the rural social structure. She argues for the application of the discipline in the study of the adoption of innovations as well as in decision theory generally.

*Capital Credit.* The farmer's ability to undertake investment is said, in part, to be determined by the interest rate. In postwar economic analysis there are strong doubts that it is an important factor in businessmen's calculations. However, in agriculture it is generally accepted that even if the interest has no direct influence on investment the availability of funds does. Cowling, Metcalf, and Rayner [139] suggest that there is an inverse relationship between the interest rate and the availability of funds, but factors such as weather, government policy, the tax

[1] Some examples over a long period of time are :
M. Weber, *The Protestant Ethic and the Spirit of Capitalism,* trans. by Talcott Parsons (Scribner's, 1930); A. E. Moore and A. S. Feldman (eds) *Labour Commitment and Social Change in Developing Areas,* Social Science Research Council (New York, 1960); R. Braibanti and J. J. Spengler (eds) *Traditions, Values and Socio-Economic Development* (Duke University Press, 1961); E. E. Hagen, *On the Theory of Social Change: How Economic Growth Begins* (Dorsey, 1962).

structure and technical factors are also important. Many studies have considered that investment in agriculture is constrained by the availability of funds because of forms of tenure, but a major problem, it is alleged, is an institutional one in that there is no central market for agricultural credit. Thus the farmer has to rely on his own income or the commercial banking system. This is probably only true of the United Kingdom, for on the continent of Europe and in the United States government assistance is substantial.

It would appear, therefore, that studies related to agricultural credit are either concerned with it as one determinant of investment or as a factor which alone acts as a constraint on the level of investment. In any event, since the mid-1960s the question of credit has not been the subject of rigorous or extensive study within economics as related to agriculture in industrial economies.

*Human resources.* The contribution by hired human resources to agricultural production is declining in numerical terms. This is because of the relatively small scale of farming coupled with increased capital investment and technical change, encouraged by agricultural policy. In all economies until the late 1960s hired workers represented less than 30 per cent of the total work force in agriculture. The exception was the United Kingdom where in 1968 hired labour represented 60 per cent of the total work force. Since then there has also been a discernible downward trend in the number of farmers as well as hired workers. However, the rate of decline in the numbers employed in agriculture has not kept pace with the rate of increase in output, capital substitution or pressures of technical change. The result is that agriculture is also characterised by low productivity and low incomes as well as a high rate of occupational migration.

As a consequence economists have examined the human resources in agriculture in an attempt to find the explanatory variables and to assess the effect the changes have had on agriculture itself and other sectors of the economy. There are two major areas of research interest: first, the motivations of the farmer as an entrepreneur and, second, the hired labour market, which has been studied in some detail, particularly in the United Kingdom and United States.

*The farmer as an entrepreneur.* Although it is not entirely true to allege that studies of the farmer as an entrepreneur have been generated solely as a result of the changes occurring in agriculture, research into his motivation and role in decision-making is related to the slow rate at which farmers are leaving agriculture. Examination of the entrepreneurial function in agriculture has developed from Simon's [49] general view on decision-making and later, McGuire's [45] on business behaviour. As implied above, these studies have moved in two directions. First, towards analysing the decision process by farmers as part of farm management and, second, towards seeking explanations of farmers' motivations in remaining in agriculture. The work of Thornton [52] and Dalton [6] illustrate the research done on farm management in decision-making, but it must not be forgotten that analysis of production functions and adoption of new techniques incorporate variables related to the entrepreneur. Work on motivation includes the studies by Bellerby [39], Guither [42] and Maddox [46]. Bellerby suggests that there are psychic attractions, a measure of social status and tax advantages in remaining in agriculture, but the main purpose of his book is to give reasons for low incomes and to offer remedies. Maddox's contribution to the study of the farmer is a historical review of the attempts by a succession of U.S. governments to alleviate rural poverty, while Guither examines the factors determining decisions to leave farming.

Apart from work related to innovation, the farmer's entrepreneurial activity has been poorly analysed. This is partly a reflection of the barrenness of economic analysis of the objective function of the entrepreneur, but is also due to economists' unwillingness to incorporate psychological and sociological aspects in their research, or to ignore or assume away their influence. There are signs of changes in very recent work and agricultural economists have themselves advocated sociological approaches [51]. Ruth Gasson [41] has outlined some applications of sociological principles in the economic analysis of agriculture in connection with both decision theory and farmers' motivations. She also considers that the discipline provides operational techniques, a basis for making assumptions, and that it offers explanations for vari-

34

ations in the data acquired in different studies on this aspect of agriculture.

*Hired labour.* The study of hired labour in agriculture has concentrated on the level of earnings and the rate of migration, from which research on utilisation and productivity have been generated. Two pieces of work on the labour market are worthy of note: Schuh's [150], which is an econometric analysis of the U.S. market, and Metcalf's [47] on earnings in the United Kingdom. Metcalf has also done work with Cowling on wage determination in agriculture ( see Cowling, Metcalf and Rayner [139]). The most important variables in the supply of labour are seen as the relationship between wages in agriculture and other sectors, the level of unemployment, age, education and variables representing non-income benefits. The demand for labour is a function of ratios of wages to the price of inputs, and wages to the price of outputs. Models of the determination of wages, in addition to including supply and demand variables, have incorporated profits, institutional factors, policy variables and regional variations in the variables. Such models are offered not only as explanations of low wages in agriculture, but also as a means of accounting for both the occupational migration and rate of migration of both farmers and labour [43], [50]. In addition to quantitative analyses there are many examples of more qualitative explanations leading to prescriptions for speeding up the migration process as a means of raising the level of agricultural incomes.[1] Black [40] advocates increasing the rate of release of human resources, Johnson [44] argues that there are too many resources in agriculture, therefore the marginal productivity of labour is lower than in industry and capital returns are unfavourable. Bellerby [39] includes demand factors such as low price and income elasticities for agricultural products and lack of control over the supply of products in a shrinking market. These factors are readily apparent even to the casual observer of contemporary agriculture. Often underestimated, however, are the sociological and institutional explanations of low incomes and low produc-

[1] For the E.E.C. consideration of this see *E.E.C. Projections and Plan for 1980* (Brussels, 1968).

35

tivity despite acknowledgement by economists of their existence and influence.

Newby [48], taking a sociological view, suggests that incomes are lower in agriculture because of the personal characteristics associated with farmers and workers, coupled with high job-satisfaction and the constraints imposed by the rural social structure, so that they choose to remain in agriculture.

Up to now these explanations have tended to be of an intuitive nature. Newby argues that sociologists, unlike economists, are in a position to quantify such variables. However, the idea prevails, even among sociologists, that provided the variables which explain why farmers and workers remain in agriculture can be identified, the means for encouraging migration can then be formulated and implemented. This may well be fallacious. It could be argued that agricultural incomes are low, not because the rate of migration is too slow, but because the earnings accurately reflect the level of skill and ability of those human resources in agriculture.

The influence of institutional factors on the migration and incomes problem is related to the policy measures adopted. Migration is encouraged not only as a means of raising incomes for those remaining in agriculture, but as a method of cutting the level of production and thus surpluses. It is also suggested that it will lead to an increase in the scale of farming and therefore increase efficiency. In certain areas of agricultural production this may prove to be an ill-founded proposition. Furthermore, another factor accounting for low incomes is the apparent contradiction between short- and long-run prescriptions for solving the problem. Short-run policy measures such as price support, storage and disposal of surplus output, production grants and subsidies are designed to raise farm incomes, and as a result tend to offset forces pushing farmers and workers out of the industry. This line of inquiry has hardly been pursued by agricultural economists.

Apart from work on the explanatory variables, the agricultural labour market has interested economists because of the effect on the other sectors of the economy. It is argued that the agricultural labour force constitutes a pool of human resources which can be absorbed into industrial sectors and thus contribute to

36

economic growth. In a study of the O.E.C.D. countries, K. Cowling and D. Metcalf ('Labour Transfer from Agriculture: A Regional Analysis', *Manchester School of Economics and Social Studies*, Mar 1968) analysed this in conjunction with an examination of the determinants of migration and made observations on both farming and industry in the regions. The results were inconclusive, partly because they concentrated on the determinants of migration and partly because it proved difficult to link migration with growth. Another approach has been the comparison of the growth rates of countries with agricultural work forces of different proportions. For example, it has been pointed out that the United Kingdom's growth potential is much lower than Italy's because it has virtually released, to other sectors, its surplus human resources in agriculture. N. Kaldor, in *Causes of the Slow Rate of Growth of the United Kingdom* (Cambridge University Press, 1966), took this view, suggesting that the secondary sector suffered a shortage of labour as a result and this not only curtailed growth but also contributed to wage inflation.

The question of remedies for improving the position of human resources in agriculture *vis-à-vis* other sectors is examined further in Chapters 2 and 3 on policy (pp. 53, 56 ff.).

### (c) Market structure

Analysis of the market structure [62], [63], [68] in agriculture, in its widest sense includes production functions and the farm firm, the grading, processing and distribution of output (incorporating also the form of competition), the effect on agricultural markets of government policy and the examination of demand [66]. Some of the characteristics of agricultural production, both at individual and market level, have already been given in the section on supply (pp. 8 ff.) and the effect of demand on the marketing of output is inspected below in the section on demand in this chapter (p. 46). This leaves, for consideration here, the marketing process of agricultural output (which includes distribution) and the structure of that process in terms of the form of competition. Indeed, following the rationale of surveying recent work in the field, these two areas square with current interest, although the examination of market structure does shade off into agricultural policy.

Elementary references on economics usually introduce concepts of perfect competition by outlining, as a classic example, the characteristics of the market for agricultural products. The assumptions of many small units, free to enter and leave the market, competing against each other to sell a homogeneous good at a given price to many buyers, is an oversimplification. The importance of the farmer as a price-taker who contributes to instability in agricultural marketing is not denied, but if the chain from production to retailing is inspected more closely, together with a differentiation of commodities, then agriculture does not appear as such a clear example of a perfectly competitive model. Moreover, the impact of the factor markets on output marketing is often overlooked, for the price of inputs to farmers depends on the structure of the industry supplying the particular input and its efficiency. For example, the supply of fertilisers could be said to be via an oligopolistic structure.

If the production of particular agricultural products is examined there are distinct elements of imperfect competition; both in the United Kingdom and the United States the broiler industry is characterised by a substantial degree of concentration [65]. At the distribution stage the tendency for some products to be marketed via contracts or some kind of marketing board system gives rise to the possibilities of monopsony from the farmers' point of view and monopoly as far as the consumer is concerned. Thus, at a number of points along the chain the activities of industries and bodies affected by forces outside agriculture exert pressures within it. At a purely theoretical level agricultural economists analyse the determination of price, the degree of competition, market efficiency, the effect of technical change, differences in scale and costs and profits, by drawing on the vast body of more general economic analysis of the firm and industry.[1] At a more empirical level economists have concentrated their attention on the pattern and effect of changes in marketing. The major interests of analysis are :

(i) production, processing and distribution costs with particular reference to variations in the margins which farmers obtain on their output; and

[1] See Metcalf [3a] for a succinct account of economic theory applied to agriculture in this context.

(ii) the methods of marketing, what might be called 'market constructions', such as the co-operatives, marketing boards, contract schemes and the more traditional outlets such as auctioning and direct selling to the public.

These interests largely reflect wider concern over the relative performance of agriculture and, moreover, show that marketing and agricultural policy are inextricably mixed. Findings on the structure and functioning of agricultural markets influence policy decisions and at the same time the operation of markets is often determined by the measures instituted by the central government – the instance of marketing boards has already been cited. Therefore, in examining agricultural and related markets, some discussion of agricultural policy is unavoidable, but attention is drawn to further appraisal of markets in Chapter 3 on policy (pp. 59 ff.).

Of the work on market structure, research in the United States has taken a somewhat different direction from that in Europe. The framework of analysis outlined by Clodius and Mueller [55] echoed the attitudes towards business in the United States on concepts of workable competition, but their work also influenced the orientation of studies towards establishing the degree of competition in various commodity markets. In a sense this related applied work much more closely to the underlying economic theory. However, it accentuated the problems where the methodology and data were inadequate for the task [58]. In Europe, particularly in the United Kingdom, study of margins and the marketing process has figured more prominently in applied work in establishing the good and bad features of the existing markets and suggesting how performance might be improved [69].

(i) *Production, processing and distribution.* The study of margins reveals that the percentage of the final price of commodities accruing to the farmer has steadily declined. The inference, then, is that processing and distributive margins have increased, but there is no evidence to support this argument. There is a wealth of data in the United States on margins at the various stages of distribution and a number of studies have been undertaken in the United Kingdom on particular markets, notably meat, eggs, and milk [38], [53], [59], [61]. Graham Hallett

39

([78], ch. 9) has summarised some studies and indicates reasons for the trends, and also discusses the stabilising effect of distributors on market prices in the same way as dealers in futures even out fluctuations where supply varies over a considerable range.

The significance of changes in grading, processing and distribution patterns lies in changing demand patterns and the increased handling of commodities has, as a consequence, increased costs. In the United States location of production has been studied quite extensively. Obviously, compared with most European countries, transport costs form a considerable proportion of total distribution costs and thus exploitation of possible comparative advantages, due to location, is worth considering. Prescriptions for improving the margin at the production stage include devices to cut down handling and speed up the distribution of products, tinkering with the institutional arragements in the market, improving the flow of information to buyers and sellers, and differentiation of the product. A closer inspection of these prescriptions is one key to the trend of studies to return to consideration of the form of competition and degree of concentration in agriculture. J. D. Shaffer ('Changing Orientations of Marketing Research', *American Journal of Agricultural Economics*, vol. 50, no. 5, Dec 1968) suggests that in the United States interest is now focused on market institutions and agricultural subsectors.

(ii) *Methods of marketing.* An important feature of some agricultural marketing has been the integration of processes as a means of controlling costs. Alongside this there has also been a movement towards the concentration of production of certain commodities. The classic case is that of broiler production, and Roy's [65] article on competition in the production of this commodity acts as an illustration of this type of study. The broiler industry is characterised by low costs and margins, a high rate of technological exploitation and a propensity to integration and concentration [64]. Other subsectors of agriculture have begun to display the same characteristics without the tendency to integration; they rely on contracting as the link between production and distribution [54].

Examples are fruit- and vegetable-growing, sugar-beet, and

40

some grain products where, although it can be argued that producers are independent, they are subject to the pressures of large buyers, as, at the distribution level at least, concentration has occurred. These trends towards integration and concentration have merely brought back into prominence a factor in marketing which has existed since the First World War in the form of co-operatives and marketing boards. Experience in the United States with co-operatives has encouraged work on its theoretical aspects [60] whereas, despite the long history of commodity marketing boards in the United Kingdom, examination of them has been weighted towards the beneficial effect of their role from a farmer's point of view, rather than their theoretical underpinnings and the welfare loss suffered by the consumer. The function of marketing boards, Cohen [56], Davies [57] and Warley [67], is seen as a means of dealing with surpluses, indicating conditions in the market, giving confidence to producers, economising on grading and processing, encouraging demand, providing credit and exercising collective control.[1] These kinds of conclusions indicate a predisposition in favour of marketing boards and a rather high degree of complacency in analysis on the part of economists. However, in recent years the efficiency and economic cost, in terms of the possible loss of consumer satisfaction and reallocation of resources, of such market organisations has been called in question from a different direction. This has occurred because of the perceived effect on member countries – and those trading with them – of E.E.C. agricultural policy. In the United Kingdom a number of studies have been undertaken which tried to assess the likely effects on British agriculture of the Common Agricultural Policy (C.A.P.), in the event of the United Kingdom's entry into the E.E.C. [72], [83]. The studies tended to take a comparative approach on the market systems and differing policies for agriculture, but the likelihood of entry also led to a reappraisal of British policy on marketing. In the conclusions drawn on the impact of the required changes in British policy one can detect the continued adherence to the view that U.K. policies on marketing are superior. Discussion of this point moves the examina-

[1] The reader is invited to look at marketing boards in the light of the economic theory on discriminating monopoly.

tion of marketing margins and organisations towards the appraisal of pricing policies, and this is considered below in Chapters 3 and 4.

### (d) The nature of uncertainty

The effect of uncertainty in relation to agriculture has already been touched on at a number of points; in the examination of farmers' reactions to supply conditions, the analysis of production functions, the adoption of innovations and the decision-making role of the farmer himself. The nature of uncertainty discussed here, in some respects, brings together for examination those aspects in a more general context.

An idea of the basic view of uncertainty in agriculture can be gained from the determinants included in supply functions. Assumptions are made about the farmer's objective function, usually profit maximisation, and then variables on the farmer himself, such as expectations on output and prices, are incorporated. These functions have also considered uncertainty outside the farmer's control, such as the effects of technical change and variations in yields. A number of studies in economic literature have also analysed at length the methodological framework in which uncertainty can be included. A great deal of work in economics, both at a theoretical and applied level, has grown from J. von Neumann and O. Morgenstern's work on the theory of games *The Theory of Games and Economic Behaviour* (Princeton, 1944). At the management and planning level, in the late 1960s, there was a proliferation of work based on this approach on the overall decision process and in connection with particular commodities. Hazell's work is an example of the use of game theory applied to farm planning, and Agrawal and Heady [102] discuss various models and possible applications to agriculture at a rather more general level than Hazell [106]. Dillon's [103] article is an earlier contribution to a review of the state of knowledge in a more critical tone.

It would appear that the work has taken two directions: towards identification of its salient features within what could be called the 'agricultural milieu' in one case, and the farmer and his concept of and ability to cope with it in the other. There are four main areas within the milieu where uncertainty is encountered :

1, the possible technical feasibilites,
2, in connection with output levels,
3, in the product and factor markets, and
4, within the political and social structure.

*Technical feasibilities.* Something has already been said about the uncertainty surrounding the selection of enterprises and allocation of resources in a farm business due to unforseeable fluctuations in product and resource prices. Adaption to these fluctuations depends on flexibility in the farm structure and the possibilities of diversification and the rate of technical change. The corn-growing belt in the United States has found it very difficult to substitute other crops, let alone move into animal husbandry. The small farms in the West Country in the United Kingdom could not specialise in say barley production without extensive changes in farm size and layout, and huge expenditure on capital equipment. Johnson [107] has likened the problems of diversification in agriculture to investment portfolio selection (see also Markowitz [108] in a much earlier and general study). Work on flexibility of enterprises and diversification suggests that smaller farmers would benefit as risks would be spread as well as allowing a margin of safety where uncertainty exists. This is at odds with other pressures which are moving agriculture towards specialisation in larger units and increased capitalisation through technical change. Up to now the information available to economists enables explanations to be offered as to why farmers diversify, without necessarily showing that there are sound economic reasons for doing so.

*Output levels.* Factors which give rise to uncertainty are those which determine yields. These are the quality of the inputs (related to technical improvements), the incidence of pests and diseases, and the weather. However, the incidence of pests and diseases is neither independent of the quality of the input nor the weather. Prima facie it would seem logical that to improve and safeguard yields a farmer should increase the quantity of inputs. For example, he could make entensive use of pesticides or heavier applications of fertiliser. On this basis uncertainty is a function of costs, but it has already been stated that this sort

43

of operation is subject to the law of diminishing returns. There is also evidence that the factors interact so as to increase uncertainty as to yields. For example, improved strains of wheat require a greater, not lesser, application of fertiliser, and they can be more susceptible to pests and plant diseases. Because the technical knowledge is incomplete it could be argued that uncertainty is increased by the very improvements designed to reduce it. As a result, this also confounds economic analysis which is attempting to construct strategies for dealing with uncertainty. The effect of weather on output has exercised American economists: Shaw [109] has analysed the effects of weather on output and Doll [105] has attempted to devise a technique for estimating indices of weather. The success of these attempts depends on the reliability and extent over time of the data, and the assumptions about the stability of climatic patterns. So far, inferences of an economic nature on this factor are really a function of the methodological framework.

*Product and factor markets.* Economic analysis on uncertainty over price, particularly product prices, has gone little further than being able to identify the determinants of uncertainty and the direction of any movements. Work on market conditions has concentrated on means of controlling the market structure rather than estimating the degree of uncertainty. Such is the unpredictability of many variables that this may well be the best course of action to adopt. A fair conclusion on this aspect of 'milieu' uncertainty is that the paucity of information and the variability of the determinants has precluded the possibility of progress.

*Political and social structure.* The question which can be raised here is whether changes introduce uncertainty into agriculture. The answer is that policy changes which indirectly affect agriculture certainly do, but devices in existing agricultural legislation, at least in the United Kingdom and to some extent in the United States, make for stability because they are designed to allow for gradual changes only. In the United Kingdom relatively short-run policies, indirectly connected with agriculture, to combat inflation have affected external trade so that the prices of imported agricultural inputs has fluctuated, but direct

44

policies, such as guaranteed prices under agricultural legislation can be changed by only very small percentages over time. Farmers argue that such are the production periods that they need this kind of long-term policy stability. To reduce uncertainty surrounding overall policies estimations have to be made of trends and cyclical elements in the level of economic activity. In this sense agriculture is no different from other industrial sectors, so that more general economic analysis related to uncertainty applies.

It is worth repeating that social conditions tend to be ignored by economists either because they are viewed as being relatively stable or because they are considered irrelevant. Thus very little research on uncertainty included social factors.

The farmer has been considered quite extensively above (p. 34) with regard to the decision-making process and his adoption of new techniques, and much of the literature relating to those aspects is applicable in a more general context. The important factors making for uncertainty related to the farmer are those of a more subtle nature, such as his own characteristics, psychological make-up and his sociological milieu.

The characteristics which will determine a farmer's attitude to uncertainty, and also colour his motivation, are his age, family circumstances, education and training. An older farmer with family responsibilities and lacking education and training will have different expectations about outcomes than a younger, highly educated and trained farmer. Incorporating these factors is a recognition that subjective appraisals of uncertainty are as relevant as objectively determined values arising from the agricultural milieu. These subjective appraisals are also affected by sociological factors. The social structure and the association of farmers with each other will affect their view of uncertainty and motivation to minimise it. Together these subjective factors determine the decision a farmer will make on his strategies when faced with uncertainty. This can be illustrated by reference to the game-theory approach to uncertainty. Agrawal and Heady [102] give five models – four frequently applied in a farming context – Wald's, Laplace's, Savage's, Hurwicz's and one of their own called the 'benefit criterion'. Each model has different payoffs and it is readily apparent that the characteristics of the individual will determine the choice, even though the payoffs may be objectively determined. Dixon [104] implies that methods form part of the information given to farmers and the reliability of the information in part determines uncertainty. Social psychologists and sociologists go further and state that economists continue to underestimate the influence of personal and social factors, and therefore the degree of uncertainty is greater than it would be if these factors were given more weight. This theme recurs in considering the conditions of demand, to which attention is now turned.

## 2 DEMAND

It is not the intention here to dwell on demand in connection with agriculture. On a theoretical level there is no difference in the analytical methods employed for general analysis and those applied to agriculture. Much of the empirical work is also common. Indeed, the demand for food is one of the most worked-over areas in economics. The procedure adopted here is to sketch in the theoretical background, indicate the definitive references on that background, consider the parts which are relevant and of most concern to agriculture and then examine some of the recent studies.

The important determinants of demand given in basic texts – price, income, the price of other goods, population and tastes – give a superficial view of demand, and often the empirical reference is weak. However, some of the pioneering analytical studies of household budgets are extremely searching, both on substantive and methodological planes. These budget analyses concentrated on the establishment of consumption patterns and calculation of elasticities rather than the effect of demand on the determination of market price. The findings of the original work by Engel [25] and the early study by Allen and Bowley [22] have been reinforced by Prais and Houthakker [29], [34] (both together and individually) and Leser [32], although there has been a tendency for these studies to get involved in the methodological problems. Related to the budget studies is the body of research on the consumption function; Ackley [21, ch. 10] has produced

46

an excellent summary of the major theories on consumption up to the late 1960s.

The budget studies have examined consumption patterns both over time, mainly in an attempt to measure the effect of price changes on demand, and on a cross-sectional basis, where the demand patterns within different regions, income groups, socio-economic classes, age groups, household composition and even ethnic groups, can be analysed. The most important conclusions of the studies are that as income rises the proportion spent on food declines, the proportion on housing is relatively stable but the proportion on clothing and luxuries tends to increase. However, within the general trends on food expenditure there is considerable variation in the kind of food consumed. Higher income groups consume more meat and fresh fruit and vegetables than lower income groups in which the proportion of total expenditure on carbohydrates is higher.

Most consumption function studies try to reconcile perceived discrepancies in expenditure and income between cross-section and time-series analysis. For example, J. S. Duesenberry (*Income Saving and the Theory of Consumer Behavior* (Harvard University Press, 1949)) suggests that it stems from the basic characteristics of different ethnic and income groups offering a semi-sociological explanation, whereas M. Friedman (*A Theory of the Consumption Function* (Princeton University Press, 1957)), relates it to a notion of 'permanent' income as the crucial determinant of expenditure level rather than current or past income (see Ackley [21] for a discussion of these theories).

The present state of the knowledge of expenditure patterns and consumer behaviour is patchy because the available data are incomplete and, of rather more fundamental importance, the methodology is somewhat threadbare. There have been some excursions into psychology (Katona [30]) and sociology (Burk [24]) to establish how habits and tastes form and are changed, and there have been rather localised studies of households in attempts to overcome the problems associated with data. However, on the whole it is at a theoretical level that there is a continuing debate and almost as a consequence empirical work seems to ignore theoretical considerations and be largely descriptive [28].

From agriculture's point of view progress in the identification of significant variables and an understanding of their relationship with each other would prove invaluable. Notwithstanding the uncertainty surrounding agricultural production, the type of food products, the level of output, marketing and the resources retained in agriculture all depend on accurate forecasts of demand patterns and consumption levels. This is certainly true of the short term and relatively long term for both developing and industrial nations. The establishment of the inelastic nature of the demand for most food products, with respect to income, and the trend towards protein products when projected with the growth of income and population, yield the direction of future consumption patterns and levels only in terms of broad orders of magnitude. For planning agricultural activity more precise and detailed estimates are essential, but of the few examples in the United Kingdom (see Ball *et al.* [23] and Williams [38]), and the rather more numerous ones in the United States [27], [37], (Kuznets [31], an early study, and Rojko [35] are given as examples; see also O.E.C.D. [33] and F.A.O. [26] projections (for production and consumption) there are none which would have any real operational significance).

It may well be that the difficulties with variables, such as population and income projections, outside those directly concerned with data and methodology, compound the problems encountered in making precise estimates, but as Slater [36] quite rightly states, the data are often highly aggregative and thus virtually useless for planning at a lower level. There are further complications associated with consumption and agricultural activity which have not been examined but should be noted. These are the demand for farm products for consumption on the farm or as inputs for other products on both an intra- and inter-farm level, the trade in food products and the effects of government policy.

# 2 Government Policy and Agriculture: I

## 1 CHARACTERISTICS OF AGRICULTURE

This and the following chapters ought to be viewed as one, for the separation of material is really for the sake of convenience. The characteristics of agriculture, which seem to warrant and have led to intervention, and the objectives and the methods adopted for their achievement are considered first. An attempt is then made to summarise the work done on the principal policies adopted by industrial nations, including the observations made by economists on the effect of these policies on the agricultural sector. Some elements of the policies are also of importance at the point where the effect of agriculture on other sectors is examined, so that there is a link to Chapter 4. In effect the more theoretical basis of policy is outlined before moving to an empirical reference.

The appraisal of work on policy can be initiated by a re-examination of some of the material given in the previous chapter which referred to the influence of policy measures.

In the sections on the elasticity of supply and demand both the inelasticity of demand and the variation in the supply of many products from period to period were stressed; this led to instability and a tendency for production cycles to result. The sequence is for fluctuating prices to give rise to changes in revenue and income of considerable magnitude,[1] which in turn is said to disrupt the pattern of production and create a greater degree of uncertainty (see p. 10). Thus one reason for interfering with the

[1] See R. Bennett Jones, 'Stability in Farm Incomes', *Journal of Agricultural Economics*, vol. 20, no. 1 (1969), where a measure of income variability revealed that the variation of incomes in agriculture appears to be twice that in other sectors but that price variation was a poor indicator of changes in income.

industry is to iron out *fluctuations* in agricultural prices and incomes.

Although the factors which give rise to fluctuations have some effect on the general *level* of incomes, the most important influences have been technical change (p. 30) and the slow rate of migration (p. 35) of resources from agriculture. Associated with technical change are the degree of specialisation and the pressures to increase the scale of farming despite more recent signs of a limit to these. As a concomitant the rate of change in farm structure and land-use are very slow due to their physical characteristics and the institutional constraints imposed on them. The rate of migration of human resources applies to both farmers and hired workers; explanations of the rate were offered on page 35. The effect of such variables is that the supply of agricultural products continually outstrips the demand for them, resulting in food surpluses and persistently low incomes.[1] This has induced governments to institute policies akin to those adopted for regions where unemployment is higher than the national average as the root causes are similar.

In a number of industrial economies agriculture is characterised by an apparent inability to compete with the agricultural sectors of other countries, and therefore, as already outlined, the tendency for incomes to fluctuate and be lower than they might be is reinforced. This may merely reflect the existence of comparative advantage elsewhere and should not give rise to concern on purely economic grounds, but many factors complicate the situation and indeed *can* cause agriculture to display what amounts to features of comparative *dis*advantage where none may have existed before. For example, in the United Kingdom the tax and legal structures have tended to favour the retention of resources in agriculture which have lowered its efficiency. Countries with a comparative advantage often support their agriculture in order to extend their markets further or to overcome trade barriers both natural and artificial. Policies related to other industrial sectors, social factors and historic reasons add to the complications, which tend to distort what might be considered to be the natural workings of economic mechanisms.

[1] In the United States usually referred to as rural poverty.

50

Many economists [2a], [3a], [78], have argued that the market structure of agriculture (see p. 37), although ostensibly approaching the theoretical ideal of perfect competition, operates in such a way as to give rise to the characteristics outlined above, and thus warrants intervention for purely economic reasons. Others go further, still on economic grounds, suggesting that intervention is justified for one or more of the contributions agriculture makes to economic growth [1], [94], [101] see pp. 29 ff.) the improvement in the balance of payments through its import-saving role [75], [94], [95] (Chapter 3, p. 62), in meeting the demand for food in the future because of rising population and for strategic reasons in times of war. Arguments of an economic nature, but with political overtones, are also put forward to justify intervention. For example, it is argued that it is necessary in order to mitigate the effects of past policies on trade and those relating to economic stabilisation, or structural changes in other sectors of the economy which affect or are affected by the agricultural sector.

If the social and political reasons based on welfare and equity, such as cheap food policies, the preservation of rural life and protection of minority groups, are added to this list economic analysis of agriculture's position becomes extremely complex as the number of objectives and their supportive policy measures multiply. One observation, however, can be made with certainty : the economic rationale for instituting agricultural policies is very difficult to establish if one subscribes to a free market view of the industry. Indeed, very few, if any, economists have taken such a purist approach; but even allowing for a modified view which sees agriculture as being parallel to that for assisting certain regions, some of the arguments of an economic nature appear to be very dubious. For example, it is very difficult to justify agriculture's import-saving role and contribution to growth. Before these arguments are examined further, however, a brief description of the policy instruments should be added to the reasons cited for intervention.

# 3  POLICY INSTRUMENTS

The policies adopted can be classified into :
- (*a*) short run – largely price support acting on ouput,
- (*b*) long run – almost exclusively structural and designed to influence inputs.

These are broad divisions as in some cases pricing policies under the guise of market structure policies are often advocated and implemented as long-run solutions to problems.

## (*a*) Short-run policies

These are seen as a means of trying to iron out fluctuations in, and raise the level of, farm incomes as an end in itself or as part of other objectives such as the expansion of the agricultural sector. The policies take two forms : (i) those which attempt to modify the market price at the time of sale or recompense farmers if they sell at a price in the free market below that considered adequate, and (ii) those which are given at the production stage.

The following list is illustrative rather than exhaustive:

(i) *Market policies.* I. Target/intervention/threshold prices (the basis of the Common Agricultural Policy (C.A.P.) involving support buying to hold up the market price). II. A deficiency payment, linked to a guaranteed price; formerly used in the United Kingdom. It allows the product to be sold at a 'freely determined market price', and should this be below the guaranteed price the difference will be made good by the deficiency payment. III. Controls on imports of food products; levies, tariffs and quotas which tend to maintain or raise the price of home-produced food commodities. IV. Buffer stocks held by some kind of government agency which comes into the market to undertake support buying when output is greater than that which will clear the market at an agreed price. The surplus is stored and released when output falls and market price is higher than the price considered desirable. V. Modification to the market structure; this usually involves the setting up of co-operatives or marketing boards which introduce restrictions on output and set minimum standards and prices. Grading of the product and separation of markets makes price discrimination possible. Boards often fulfil the functions given under IV.

Of a more intermediate nature are : VI. Land banks, production quotas, licences, etc, which have the effect of reducing the level of output with the intention of raising the market price.

(ii) *Production stage policies*. These amount to variations on a theme of those policies given in (i), for the devices are designed to increase farm income by reducing costs at the farm level. The intention, assuming a given market price, is that profit margins will rise, increase farm incomes and thus encourage expansion of production.

Many measures take the form of grants for fixed and variable capital inputs. For example, in the United Kingdom there are grants for drainage, farm buildings, power and fuel, which lead to the expansion of production of agricultural products generally. Others are specific grants to encourage production of particular commodities such as beef-cow subsidies or fertilisers for arable crops. The idea of production grants is to subsidise the farmer direct rather than via the market, the assumption being that the policy is distinct and more effective.

The similarities in the effect of market policies and production grants is discussed in Chapter 3.

## (b) Long-run policies

The immediate aim of long-run policies is to reinforce short-term goals, but the ultimate objective is to achieve those which improve the efficiency of agriculture and so obviate the need for price support as well as contributing to the overall efficiency of the economy. Economic considerations are modified by social desiderata so that, as with short-run policies, instruments are an amalgam of economic and other aims.

One example of a policy which is intermediate in form, in terms of its impact lag, has already been given above. Another which might be viewed as such is: I. Research, advisory work and training and education – the expected effect is relatively long-term; therefore it can be usefully classified under this heading. Policies which relate to advice and training involve supporting information services, employing agricultural advisers, maintaining training centres and colleges and financing research at universities. They are also designed to improve the efficiency of all the resources utilised in agriculture in contrast to policies of more recent origin, designed to push resources out of the industry. II. Migration policies – these are devices which both push and pull resources out of agriculture. They tend to concentrate on human resources, and examples are retraining, education, retirement payments, supply of information on opportunities in other sectors, resettlement grants and land reform. Generally speaking, the forces acting on agriculture have encouraged migration of hired labour without recourse to policy measures. It is the farmer who has caused most concern, but even here there are 'natural' forces at work so that policy is aimed at varying the rate of migration. The aim of most measures is to raise the incomes of those remaining in agriculture although it is thought that efficiency will also increase as a result. III. Farm structure changes – the rather complex economic relationships between tenure, size, layout, specialisation, scale, factor combination and technical change have been outlined in Chapter 1. The policies tend to reflect this complexity by being uncertain in their application. They range from land reform connected with tenure and size and amalgamation of units to providing credit facilities, capital grants, incentives to adopt new practices and tax exemptions and remissions. IV. Market structure changes – although examined under short-run price-support measures, certain market policies are intended to improve agricultural efficiency. Two of the most favoured measures are those which attempt to raise farm incomes by reducing the costs of moving food products from the farmer to the consumer, and those making agriculture more competitive. Integration, co-operatives and marketing boards are alleged to achieve both these aims with the threat of intervention by governments where there might be the elements of monopoly. For example, in the United Kingdom recommendations were made to set up supervisory development authorities in meat marketing to combat monopolistic tendencies arising out of proposals for marketing boards. V. Regional development – a number of countries, notably the United States and the continental E.E.C. countries, have policies of this nature which include agriculture. Reference has already been made to the similarities between structural changes in basic extractive and manufacturing industries and agriculture; the problem of rural poverty becomes a regional one where particular areas are predominantly agricultural. The grounds for intervention are social rather than economic, and the measures are both short- and long-run, since they involve price and income support as interim measures, and structural reform as the ultimate means of effecting changes.

The examination of short- and long-run policies here has necessarily been extremely scanty. For a fuller description reference should be made to publications by Hallett [78], Rasmussen and Baker [92], the O.E.C.D. [88], Iowa State University Center [81], Nash [86] Papi and Nunn [19] and the general bibliography, section A is recommended.

Having outlined the *apparent* reasons for, and the methods of, intervention, the next step is to consider the effects on the agricultural and other sectors of the economy, at the same time commenting on the related literature.

# 3 Government Policy and Agriculture: II

It is appropriate to summarise the effects of agricultural policy. This will facilitate discussion and serve as a vehicle for examination of the contribution made by economics and economists in this particular field. Little attempt will be made to analyse the relative merits of each measure in detail since lack of space precludes this. Therefore the approach is illustrative and somewhat sketchy.

Study of the history and application of agricultural policy leads to four observations on its effects :

(*a*) Short- and long-run goals and their associated policy measures contradict each other.

(*b*) There is a transfer of incomes and resources to agriculture.

(*c*) Economic costs are imposed on other sectors of the economy.

(*d*) International trade in food products between countries is lower than it might have been.

The effect of (*a*) can be said to result in (*b*) and (*c*); whereas (*d*) is the consequence of specific policies, the express intention of which is to restrict trade in certain commodities.

There are naturally some qualifications to these bald statements which need to be noted :

(i) They require verification by reference to theoretical and empirical evidence.

(ii) Even if made on economic grounds alone they imply that, as a result of policy, agriculture has departed from some theoretical ideal. This should not be pushed too far as one very quickly runs up against the arguments related to the theory of second-best.

(iii) They underestimate or ignore non-economic criteria by which agricultural policy should be judged. For example, there are social costs in allowing the industry to run down.

56

Notwithstanding these qualifications it is remarkable to what extent agriculture has been protected, especially in the light of recent and more searching academic scrutiny of the industry. As an example of the degree of protection afforded by policy, identifiable[1] exchequer support in the United Kingdom forms a very substantial part of the total net farm income; that is to say, much of the net income of the industry has been provided by the government.

Support of this magnitude is common in many other countries, notably the United States. Prima facie it would appear to be far greater than is warranted by the circumstances. To see why protection has been taken so far it is necessary to appreciate the development of industrial economies and the rationale of agricultural policy. This is not pursued here, although a number of elements are traced in order to illustrate some points of importance. For a comprehensive treatment of agricultural policy see the texts by Hallett [78], Hathaway [79], Paarlberg [90] Rasmussen and Baker [92], Schickele [96] and Tracy [100]. The effects of the First World War seemed to have imprinted two thoughts on the minds of farmers and governments. First, the acute shortages during the war, and second the wild fluctuations in prices immediately following it, with subsequent price collapse as production recovered. Thus support was readily agreed after the Second World War, largely for strategic and economic reasons, with the objective of stabilising prices, raising incomes and encouraging expansion of production. As a corollary import restrictions were imposed in many European countries as an additional means of supporting domestic agriculture. Although there were tentative applications of structural policies based on vague ideas that they would improve efficiency and lead to higher levels of output, the indecisiveness over encouraging structural changes was a reflection of the lack of knowledge of the type of measures required and the time period over which they would take effect. Because support

[1] This means that hidden subsidies – for example, the effect of raising the market price of home-produced products by preventing the import of the same commodities produced more cheaply abroad – are not included. If they were it is possible that total subsidies would equal or exceed total net income.

57

policies had a more immediate impact, they prevailed; there was also a political element in this which is examined below.

Once the food shortages were overcome it quickly became apparent that the underlying pattern of continued industrialisation, begun in the nineteenth century, would be maintained. This was accompanied by an even greater comparative advantage in manufacturing industries, while rapid technical innovation occurred in agriculture, so depressing farm incomes despite the increasing rate of migration. This exacerbated the agricultural sector's problems. It seemed that even more support would be required to maintain the industry and achieve the desired goals. It ought to be noted that this outline of trends is somewhat general as conditions in different countries varied. For example, United States governments recognised the need and introduced structural changes sooner, and, of the European countries, the United Kingdom, through former policies of free trade and earlier industrialisation, had a lower work-force and a potentially more efficient farm structure.

Economists can approach the analysis of policy on two levels: either they examine the policy objectives and consider the effect of these, or they accept the objectives as given and examine the effect of the various means of attaining them. The differing emphasis of economists studying the agricultural sector has been noted in Chapter 1, and nowhere is this more apparent than in analysis of policy. Those brought up in an agricultural tradition are apt to be committed to the latter approach, though some more general economists are not entirely unaffected. T. Josling [82], in an excellent analysis of the effect of various support measures, accepts the goals as given, although in a footnote he recognises the need to question them but then accents problems of venturing into an area overgrown by a political jungle. Some of the texts on policy are extremely mild in criticising the goals, for example, Hallett [78], Iowa State University Center [81] and Schickele [96]. Certainly those working in specific areas of study in agriculture, such as marketing, market structure, the human resources, growth and trade, ought to show concern for objectives but so often do not. Therefore, the biggest gap in the literature, at least until the late 1960s, was that which concerned fundamental policy issues. Notable exceptions are the relatively early studies of policy by Allen [70], McCrone [83] and Nash [86], who considered the place of agriculture and the policy objectives in a rigorous and detached manner.

Against this background attention is now turned to the observations summarised at the beginning of this chapter; the first three, (a)–(c), may be usefully considered together.

The theoretical evidence on interference in the market through the devices of :

(i) restricting supply,

(ii) setting price above the free-market equilibrium, and

(iii) paying market or production subsidies,

can be found in any elementary book on economics. Josling [82] gives a diagrammatic exposition of the effects of different forms of agricultural support related to import-saving and the transfer of income to the farm sector, and compares the cost of the alternative means of attaining these aims. He concludes that the deficiency payment policy is the most effective in achieving income transfer, but that a mixed system would be more efficacious if the object were to save foreign exchange. As the United Kingdom has pursued both a policy of import-saving and income transfer, and in the past, employed deficiency payments as means, Josling's observations are apposite. Fig. 4 illustrates the

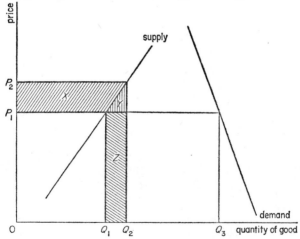

Fig. 4  The effect of a deficiency payment on farm income and the import of food

59

arguments put forward by Josling on the use of deficiency payments and the figure is based on that appearing in his article. If the world price of the commodity is $P_1$, domestic supply is $0Q_1$ and domestic demand is $0Q_3$. To reduce the level of imports of the commodity, which is equivalent to $Q_1$, $Q_3$, and increase farm incomes, a subsidy equal to $P_1$, $P_2$ is applied. The level of output is equal to $0Q_2$ and the result of the policy is that imports are reduced by $Q_1$, $Q_2$. This means that foreign exchange equal to the shaded area of $Z$ has been saved, but the deficiency payment is equal to the shaded areas $X$ and $Y$.

It is clear from Fig. 4 that the methods of interfering in the market have the effect of retaining or diverting into agriculture resources which might otherwise have been utilised elsewhere, as well as encouraging expansion of production.[1] These conclusions are valid on the basis of assumptions about elasticities of demand and supply made in Chapter 1 which are supported by a large body of empirical evidence. McFarquhar and Evans [84] have summarised projections on the demand for food products and the references on production and supply functions give supply elasticities.

Both demand and supply elasticities are given in general texts on policy. Although theoretical analysis suggests it, evidence that resources are retained or diverted into agriculture is more difficult to establish at an empirical level. Measurement of the productivity of agriculture constitutes one approach with a view to making a comparison with that in manufacturing industry (Ministry of Agriculture, Fisheries and Food [13], Cowling, Metcalf and Rayner [139]). Another approach is to consider the factor rewards of agriculture with its contribution to national income. In agriculture, calculating either of these measures is complicated by the operation of the very policy of which an evaluation is being sought. Nevertheless, there is sufficient evidence [83] to conclude that policy has distorted the allocation of resources despite the express intention of expanding agriculture. (See also the references which examine factor shares by Bell-

[1] It may seem paradoxical that restriction of supply should lead to expansion of production, but consider the long-run effect of the consequent price rise on the production plans of farmers when no absolute bar on output levels is imposed, which is the case with many supply restriction devices.

erby [39], Metcalf [47], Stout and Rattan [50] and the discussion on capital and human resources in Chapter 1).

Observation that incomes are lower in agriculture compared with other sectors is in itself an indication that there are too many resources in the industry. Taking the U.K. case, the slow working of the factor market is often quoted as a reason for low earnings, and social investigations support this view. However, those who account for low incomes as due to technical change, increasing scale and factor substitution, and by showing how high labour productivity has been are incredibly naïve. Evidence on the productivity of *all* resources in agriculture indicates that it is generally lower than in manufacturing industries (Clark [4], Peters [16]). Indeed, by viewing the statistics on productivity alongside those on the individual factors it is possible that the productivity of capital has been negative. Furthermore, if allowance is made for the favourable effect of the tax structure and policy – for example, production grants as a means of reducing costs of incentives to improve efficiency through specialisation – the performance of agriculture would have been even poorer. Suggestions that there is an inevitable lag as the result of a policy of expansion are not borne out by the evidence.

An argument of a different shade is that there are more resources in agriculture than appear to be required, but that this is the inevitable consequence of policies concerned with import-saving and agriculture's contribution to growth. This is because structural changes are required, but development is handicapped by the need for long-term capital investment. Sharp and Capstick [19], Dean and Carter [74], Evans [76], and Steward [99] refer to this and also the lack of credit facilities which are hampering development; this is echoed in the Iowa State University Center [81], the O.E.C.D. reports [89], and the early U.S. references by Schickele [96]. The last two sources also suggest that the tax structure militates against improved efficiency in the United Kingdom. Apart from the case in countries like Italy or parts of Germany and France, the statistics produced by Bandini *et al.* [1] bear out the conclusion drawn above that there is an increasing tendency to over-capitalisation in agriculture. There are other reasons for accepting this tendency, even if optimal factor combination had not been attained, as examination of the

61

role of agriculture in contributing to growth and in saving imports will show. The relationship between policy and growth is probably one of the most closely examined areas of all policy studies while analysis of the import-saving role, although peculiar to the United Kingdom in early post-war years, is of increasing interest to E.E.C. countries because of the nature of the Common Agricultural Policy (C.A.P.). It is alleged that for agriculture to release resources, principally labour, for employment elsewhere there needs to be a substitution of capital inputs and intensive use of land. This sort of proposition rests on two premises which may not be valid. First, that it is shortage of labour in manufacturing industries which is retarding growth, and second, that capital investment in agriculture will achieve increased output and release labour for the manufacturing industries. Clearly also, while agriculture is supplying human resources to other sectors in the economy it is demanding capital resources which could have been utilised in those other sectors. Therefore, measures of the opportunity cost of resources transferring in this way are required. A number of studies in economic literature have recognised that the quality of the human resources migrating from agriculture may not match what is required in other sectors. Farmers and workers may be too old, insufficiently educated or trained and be unwilling to rehabilitate themselves in urban areas; Galbraith [77], Hathaway [79], McCrone [83] and Shepherd [97] make this point but in the context of whether agriculture should be run down by exposure to the free-market mechanism. However, the question of which sector can make better use of capital resources when they are reallocated is of more importance. The answer, from evidence referred to above, emphatically rules against their use in agriculture.

Dissection of the case for the import-saving role of agriculture reveals that its characteristics are almost common with those for the industry's growth-contributing role. At this juncture only those aspects of the policy concerned with resource allocation are noted, the effect on trade is considered later in the section. The essence of the case in the United Kingdom is that by expanding domestic agriculture the need to import food products is reduced, thereby offsetting a balance-of-payments deficit. As far as the use of domestic resources is concerned the policy is viable only if it can be shown that the resources diverted to agriculture are more productive than they would be if they remained available for producing manufactured goods for export, or for the substitution of imported goods. The appraisal of such a policy is complicated by the need to consider the extent to which agriculture imports its raw materials to undertake expansion, e.g. feedstuffs as opposed to those materials manufacturing industry would import. The policy has been considered in times of trade crises in the United Kingdom; the report by the Economic Development Council for the Agricultural Industry [75], and Ritson's [94] article reopened a debate which Robinson [95] began in the 1950s. The controversy is unresolved because the groundwork on which a decision could be based has never been undertaken. McCrone [83], in tracing from whom imports of food products might originate, suggests that even if the groundwork was done the policy was invalid in the 1950s and 1960s because very few products which the United Kingdom could produce domestically came from outside the sterling area. Analysis of the policies which industrial nations have already applied yields sufficient empirical evidence to support those theoretical propositions that agricultural expansion imposes greater economic costs on other sectors than they in turn do on it. The analysis also supports the view that the policies have the effect of diverting resources into agriculture. Furthermore economic costs should include consideration of the social costs imposed on the respective sectors. Arguments against a diminished agricultural industry range from the deterioration in the quality of rural life and disruption of the social structure to the effects on the individual farmers and workers who need to be relocated and retrained. The arguments tend to be intuitive and the evidence is scanty, though it should be possible to devise a framework of analysis. This is also true of the social costs of maintaining or expanding agriculture at the expense of other sectors. Little beyond the enumeration of the types of cost – for example, pollution of rivers and reservoirs by fertilisers and pesticides, difficulties of access to the countryside – has been done. On a quantitative dimension the inclusion of social costs tips the balance further against agriculture. The increasing financial costs of supporting agricultural expansion borne by governments has been

recognised for long enough for objectives and policy measures to be adapted to changed conditions. As a result most industrial nations have now initiated policies which, on the one hand, continue to attempt to stabilise prices and raise incomes in agriculture, while, on the other hand, endeavouring to effect longer-term structural changes with the objectives of contracting the industry and improving efficiency. A major criticism is that neither the support nor the structural devices are appropriate to the goals. Because the support measures divert resources into agriculture they outweigh market mechanisms already forcing resources to be used more efficiently within, or be reallocated outside, agriculture. An important factor here is the inelasticity of demand for food products combined with the relatively higher elasticity of supply. Moreover, there are examples of support which achieve the opposite effect of that intended, and certainly many contradict the long-term measures. The subsidies on capital inputs which lead to the substitution of capital for labour, so creating a labour surplus and reducing incomes, is an example of the former, while small farm grants which contradict policies to improve farm structure and increase scale illustrates the latter. The articles by John Bowers and Paul Cheshire in *Decision-making in Britain: A Second-level course* – Agriculture (The Open University, 1972) examine other anomalies in U.K. agricultural policy, particularly in relation to specific policies. For example, introducing measures to discourage dairy farming in times of high beef or veal prices, and derationing animal feed-stuffs at a time when there are balance-of-payments difficulties.

Hallett [78] argues that it is not certain that support policies will slow down the rate of structural change, implying that there is no contradiction. Sociétés d'Aménagement Foncier et d'Établissement Rural [71], Cmnd 2738 [80], the O.E.C.D. [89] and Shepherd [97] all recommend amalgamation, consolidation and migration of human resources, but an earlier report by the National Resources (Technical Committee) [87] in the United Kingdom considered that there were limits to structural changes as economies of scale were not apparent above 500 acres. (Note also the technical and institutional limits mentioned in Chapter 1 (p. 32) in relation to investment.) Galbraith [77], McCrone [83] and Paarlberg [90] question the validity of abandoning support

64

policies entirely for the free-market mechanism as a method of inducing structural changes, since, from experience between the wars, it is the inefficient farmer who will remain in the industry and allow his capital assets to deteriorate to the point where it would be extremely costly to restore them. There is a danger, as Galbraith [77] quite rightly pointed out some years ago, that economic preconceptions about the market mechanism and competition and efficiency are imposed on the analysis of agricultural problems without an appreciation of their true nature. According to Hathaway [79] the values and beliefs of those in positions different from the formulators of policy are misunderstood and the political opposition to what may appear to be rational programmes underestimated. This is not true in the United Kingdom, where farmers exercise considerable influence over policy formulation (see P. Self and H. J. Storing, *The State and the Farmer* (Allen & Unwin, 1962)). However, admonishments for over-generalising the policy measures are made by Paarlberg [90] and Rickard [93] by reference to both the policy aims and goals.

Paarlberg [90], reflecting the United States' concern over integration and concentration, advocates diversification and movement, of at least part of agriculture, towards free market conditions. Rickard [93] emphasises the different goals of the member countries within the E.E.C. where more extensive structural changes are required than in the United Kingdom or the United States. He also underlines the fact that structural policies are almost non-existent on the continent of Europe. Reference to the paucity of information and the confusion over policy is also made in Butterwick and Neville-Rolfe [72], Deakin [73], Marsh and Ritson [85], Southgate [98] and Tracy [100].

Before concluding the discussion a quick look ought to be taken at the fourth observation, made on p. 56.

The theory of international trade, and an enormous body of empirical work, offers convincing evidence of the detrimental effects on the countries involved if one or more adopt measures to restrict trade. Policies by trading nations to expand domestic food production, for the reasons given above, to raise trade barriers to prevent cheaper food imports, or to save foreign exchange, lower the level of trade. The effect on resource allocation has already been outlined in connection with the U.K. import-saving policy; here the income and welfare aspects are noted.

If food imports into a country are cut because of expansion of domestic agriculture there is an increase in the incomes of the importing country, while those of the exporting country are lowered, assuming that markets are not immediately found elsewhere. This obviously reduces the ability of the food-exporting country to buy the goods of the food-importing one. If the country exporting food is a primary producer, the effect on its economy can be disastrous if it is financing the import of manufactured goods from its exports of food. Naturally there is a reciprocal effect on the country which originally cut its food imports : it loses its market for manufactured goods. Moreover there is a welfare loss in the policy-making country as high-cost food is substituted for the formerly cheaper imported food. McCrone [83] has explored at some length the idea that industrial nations might be correct in expanding domestic agriculture because food-exporting nations in the future may consume their own agricultural products as they industrialise. Thus the food-importing countries would experience food shortages and rapidly rising food prices. He concludes, by making assumptions about the rate of growth and industrialisation of primary-producing countries, that shortages are not likely to be significant for many years yet. This suggests that the welfare loss suffered at present outweighs the uncertain future gain of attempting to achieve self-sufficiency in the domestic agricultural industry in industrial nations.[1]

In the case of the United Kingdom, to the time of joining the E.E.C., the food subsidies, under a deficiency payment policy, were financed out of taxation. In future, following the Common Agricultural Policy (C.A.P.), import levies will hold the domestic market price up, thus passing the burden of the subsidy from the taxpayer to the consumer. Therefore, assuming a progressive tax structure, there is a redistribution of incomes in favour of taxpayers as well as to those in agriculture and its supporting industries. This is a highly simplified exposition of the effects; exami-

[1] Despite prognoses by those in agricultural industries of food shortages in 1975/6, as a longer-term forecast of events McCrone's view appears still to be correct.

nation of the position in particular countries involves the identification of the source and destination of tax revenues as well as the structure of agriculture and industry in analysing the reallocation of resources.

Import levies also make it more difficult to establish the respective comparative advantage and disadvantage in agriculture in the countries involved (J. Bowers, 'Efficiency in Agriculture', in *Agriculture* (The Open University, 1972)). Appraisals of the different kinds of policy are numerous. In Europe the advent of the C.A.P. and the attempts by the United Kingdom, on a number of occasions, to join the E.E.C. have generated comparative studies, such as those by Deakin [73] Southgate [98], and Tracy [100], which have a political flavour. The work by Butterwick and Neville-Rolfe [72] and Marsh and Ritson [85] have already been considered in terms of the effects on U.K. agriculture of joining the E.E.C.

The studies of the C.A.P. exemplify the level at which much of the work on policy in agricultural economics is done, where the effects of measures are analysed rather than the goals. Although there is a growing awareness of the extent to which agricultural activity impinges on other sectors and society at large, economists have hardly begun to undertake an appraisal by which new policies may be judged. There is neither an acceptable methodology nor sufficient information available to test hypotheses, so that explanations and predictions are likely to remain on an intuitive level. In widening the horizon from the examination of policy to some of the wider issues connected with agriculture, in the next chapter, these concluding remarks are equally pertinent.

# 4 Agriculture – the Wider Issues

This chapter is based largely on conditions in the United Kingdom, where the pressures for alternative uses of land are probably as great, if not greater, than elsewhere, but draws much material from studies originating in the United States.

The approach taken is to consider first some of the fundamental issues regarding rural land-use, by examining the major forms of activity other than agriculture. Then the impact of agriculture on other uses is discussed, together with the social costs the industry appears to suffer and impose. Throughout this discussion an attempt is made to interpret land-use from an economic standpoint by reference to representative studies.

## 1  MAJOR LAND-USES

These can be categorised under the following heads:
- (a)  Urban and industrial.
- (b)  Forestry.
- (c)  Water resources.
- (d)  Recreation.
- (e)  Mineral extraction and quarrying.
- (f)  Military establishments and training areas.
- (g)  Transport.
- (h)  Derelict land.

Of the uses listed, (a) will be examined, but not in any detail, while (e), (f), (g) and (h) are largely ignored, not as being unimportant, but because at an aggregative level agricultural activity has had only a marginal impact on them, and vice versa.

A valuable source of information on land-use in Britain is that by Peters [111], where he not only classifies land-use and traces the changes over time, outlining the conflict between different uses, but he also makes his own appraisal and prediction of future trends. Agriculture uses about 80 per cent of the total area of land in Great Britain but is giving it up to other uses at an average rate of about 40,000 acres per year. Table 1 indicates the major changes in land-use in Great Britain between 1900 and 1950.

TABLE 1

*Changes in the major Land-uses of Great Britain between 1900 and 1950*

(in '000 acres)

| Year | Agricultural | Woodland | Urban Development |
|------|--------------|----------|-------------------|
| 1900 | 45,340 | 2,770 | 2,170 |
| 1925 | 45,130 | 2,950 | – |
| 1935 | 45,360 | 3,210 | 3,160 |
| 1939 | 45,200 | 3,410 | – |
| 1950 | 45,240 | 3,700 | 4,070 |

SOURCE: G. H. Peters, 'Land-Use Studies in Britain', *Journal of Agricultural Economics*, vol. 21, no. 2 (May 1970) p. 176.

## (a) Urban and industrial

Misgivings over the loss of agricultural land to urban use was one of the first signs that wider issues ought to be the concern of those studying rural land-use. The work of Ward [112] and Wibberley [113] in the late 1950s has been touched on in relation to land values on p. 23 of Chapter 1 in connection with attempts to ascertain the return to land in agriculture *vis-à-vis* urban use. This is obviously also relevant to the evaluation of different rural land-uses, particularly as the authors were prompted to undertake their respective studies because they observed that good-quality agricultural land was subject to urban development and pressures were consequently being exerted on other rural land-uses. They undertook a kind of crude cost–benefit analysis of agricultural land earmarked for urban development by estimating the value in agricultural use. The method was to take the value of total output, deduct the costs of the resources used other than land, and capitalise the remaining figure. The costs of developing different sites were then related to the capitalised agricultural value

69

of each site, and, if it is assumed that in each case the agricultural values were greater than the development costs, the site which showed the lowest difference between value and cost would be developed. The approach suffered from complications related to tenure forms and associated legislative constraints, the structure of taxation and the agricultural subsidies systems, which distorted the results and led to overestimates of the value of the land in agricultural use. Furthermore, because the value in agricultural use is often quite low, any capitalised value would be sensitive to the interest rate by which it was discounted. The method adopted was not an evaluation in the true sense of the word as the loss of land to urban use, where except on social grounds the return would be virtually certain to be greater, was accepted as inevitable. M. A. B. Boddington, in a recent article ('The Evaluation of Agricultural Land in Planning Decisions', *Journal of Agricultural Economics*, vol. 24, no. 1, 1973), reconsiders the evaluation of agricultural land and suggests that land-use and non-economic criteria ought to be adopted as on no count does agriculture measure up to other uses on a purely economic basis.

Much of the analysis of the different *rural* land-uses is of a similar nature to that originally done on urban development by Ward [112] and Wibberley [113]. A few studies of the return to agriculture compared with that in forestry have worked from a common base. However, even here comparability is not always possible as there has been much methodological dispute. As for incorporating the evaluation of land for water resources and recreation, the groundwork has hardly begun on erecting a common framework of analysis. Indeed, a further problem which has not been faced squarely is evaluation where multiple use of land is possible.

### (b) Forestry

In the United Kingdom a relatively early post-war report considered forestry, agriculture and marginal land [127], and Walker [128] took up the question of whether agriculture or forestry was best suited to hill land. He also appraised the operations of the Forestry Commission. Another official report on forestry, agriculture and the multiple use of land [122] acknowledged that in certain areas land-use was not necessarily mutually exclusive. This report generated discussion on two dimensions: Openshaw [110] took up the question of methodological inconsistencies and the distorting effect of not taking account of subsidies in the calculation of the respective returns in agriculture and forestry. The other dimension paralleled the expansion and import-saving-role arguments in agriculture by examining the possibilities of substituting home-grown timber for a substantial proportion of that imported. This, naturally, would involve expansion in the home industry, and thus, it is suggested, forestry could ease unemployment in upland areas. Hampson [123] and James [124] have discussed the problems of the choice of discount rate and the timing of revenues and expenditures in a recent and continuing debate, and the Ministry of Agriculture, Fisheries and Food have made out their own case for forestry, while Lorraine-Smith [125] has evaluated the role of the private woodland-owner.

Despite strong reaction by some upland farmers against the encroachment of forestry on agricultural land, the total area of agricultural land under trees is less than 8 per cent, and, taking account of the contribution of upland farming to total agricultural output at about 5 per cent, the economic impact of this encroachment is minimal. Moreover, the contribution by forestry is about 7 per cent of the United Kingdom's total timber requirement. In value terms this was about £50 million in 1971. Therefore, neither upland agriculture nor forestry are particularly significant in economic terms. The evaluation thus seems to reduce to one which compares the return in agriculture as opposed to that in forestry, where one use excludes the other. Except at very low discount rates, notwithstanding the current debate over methodology, agriculture appears to be a better proposition whatever the quality and topography of the land.

The Forestry Commission has evidently recognised the modest role timber plays in the economy by implementing the policy which emphasises access and recreation in its lowland plantations. Thus forestry is also amenable to other uses, even assisting agriculture to some extent, and if adjustment is made for the grants and subsidies received by the respective industries, forestry should show a better return if compatible uses are incorporated. Of more serious concern for the allocation of resources in the economy as a whole is the effect on efficiency of the grants and subsidies made to forestry and upland agriculture. Questions of this nature cannot be answered until such time as there is better information and analysis of each.

### (c) Water resources

The use of rural land for water resources involves two aspects, drainage and water supply on the one hand and recreation on the other. Until now the interrelationship between agriculture and these aspects has not been recognised in the United Kingdom as it has in the United States, and consequently there are fewer studies. Concern over flood control, irrigation and soil conservation necessitated extensive research and expenditure in the United States and was instrumental in the development of cost–benefit analysis.[1] Eckstein's study [137] is an early example of the technique and Kneese and Smith [138] reflect the ensuing development. Although, in the United Kingdom the need for both flood control and irrigation are significant, they are not the most important considerations. Nor has the demand for land resources in lowland areas been an issue until recently as demand has been met from upland areas, underground sources or natural drainage. The important factors in the relationship between rural land-uses and water resources have been, first, the interaction of amenity, recreation and water supply, and, second, the problem of pollution. Both these factors are discussed below in connection with agricultural activity and social costs.

### (d) Recreation

There are a number of studies in the United States and the United Kingdom which have attempted to predict the demand for outdoor recreation in the future by making projections of demographic and socio-economic data. The Outdoor Recreation Resources Review Commission (O.R.R.R.C.) [135] made a comprehensive study of all forms of recreational activity in the United States, and less ambitious attempts have been sponsored in the United Kingdom by the Countryside Commission and the Sports Council. The British Travel Association (Pilot National Recreation Survey, University of Keele, 1969) has also

[1] See D. W. Pearce, *Cost-Benefit Analysis* (Macmillan, 1971) p. 14.

engaged in research of a similar nature to that conducted by the O.R.R.C. and the results of a study in 1965 confirm the findings in the United States.

At a lower level of generality there have been many studies on the recreational use of rural areas, most of which have concentrated on demand. These resource-based studies, as they are called, are of interest because, with the aggregative studies, they indicate the likely impact of recreation on rural land. Furthermore, a number of studies of an economic nature have endeavoured to evaluate the land if used for recreation because of competition between the alternative uses of land. A further consideration is the likelihood of the multiple use of land. One problem which has bedevilled the attempts at evaluation is the non-priced nature of most rural recreational activity. Therefore, many demand studies have concentrated on the construction of a theoretically acceptable but operational methodology in order to quantify the recreational benefit. The O.R.R.C. series of papers pioneered such approaches, and many of those who contributed to that research have since published work under their own names – for example, Clawson [130] and Clawson and Knetsch [131]. Clawson's approach, based on consumers' surplus, is probably the most fruitful economic method at present, but there are a number of points of dispute surrounding it. The method consists of constructing a demand curve by plotting the visitor rate on the vertical axis and the distance travelled on the horizontal axis. The curve slopes downwards from left to right because if the inverse relationship between visit rate and distance, where increased distance results in increased cost, in terms of both money and time. The curve gives a measure of elasticity of demand for a particular site and the area under it the value of total consumption, which can also be an evaluation of the particular resource. A number of assumptions are made about the socio-economic characteristics of the population surrounding the resource and the actual visitors, concerning their reactions to changes in cost and evaluation of time. The dispute over the method largely surrounds the evaluation of time. N. W. Mansfield, in 'Recreational Trip Generation', *Journal of Transport Economics and Policy* (May 1969), has incorporated a measure of the value of time in a model very much like the Clawson one. His approach has been criticised by M. Common, 'A Note on the Use of the Clawson Method for the Evaluation of Recreation Site Benefits', *Regional Studies*, vol. 7, no. 4 (Dec 1973), who was disturbed by the extra survey assumptions about travel times and costs.

Of the applications of the Clawson approach most have been in the United States. Burton and Noad [129] have summarised the literature on economic demand studies until the middle 1960s and the Countryside Commission have reviewed the more recent ones [132], [133]. N. J. Kavanagh, 'The Economics of the Recreational Uses of Rivers and Reservoirs', *Water and Water Engineering* (Oct 1968), and R. J. Smith and N. J. Kavanagh, 'The Measurement of Benefits of Trout Fishing', *Journal of Leisure Research* (Autumn 1969), are examples of applications of the Clawson approach to resources. They encountered problems with data, because it was of a secondary nature, and also did not deal satisfactorily with the value of time.

Apart from the methodological shortcomings of the present economic methods the main criticism of them is that they are not wide enough. Sociologists can assist analysis by identifying social trends and measuring attitudes and expectations, but there are other factors in the use of rural land. Local authority planning, management and conservation considerations impinge on the analysis of recreation which the Countryside Act (1968) emphasised in setting up the Countryside Commission in the United Kingdom.

Potential conflict with agriculture is apparent in the demand for informal recreation. Rural recreational activities necessitate access, creation of national and country parks, and the provision of picnic areas, as well as the need for land for sporting activities and long-stay recreation such as caravanning and camping, all of which intrude on agricultural activity. In turn, through economic forces, but reinforced by agricultural policy, farmers intensify their methods, which alters the landscape and cuts down the opportunity for recreation.

One consequence of efforts to cut costs in farming is a greater degree of specialisation and an increase in the scale of operations, while policy measures encourage the production of particular commodities. For example, the movement to arable farming is the result of production grants and subsidies, the technical improvement in the necessary capital equipment and discovery of new seed strains and fertilisers. Farmers bring land into culti-vation, clear scrub, trees and hedges and keep the land con-stantly in crop cultivation. Therefore recreational use of the countryside is discouraged or even prevented because the amenity or access or both cease to exist. Keenleyside [134] and Phillips and Roberts [136] outline some of the conflicts on both sides, and, although their examination of the problem is superficial, their studies form a useful starting-point for further analysis. They also indicate the difficulties in resolving the conflict, seeing the need for evaluation of different land-uses and the development of techniques at a management level, when one land-use impinges on another.

From the background which has been filled in on the alter-native uses of land it is possible to see quite clearly some of the conflicts and the obstacles which stand in the way of resolving them. Of these obstacles one of the most important is the establish-ment of a method of evaluating each type of land-use. Moreover, before priorities and policies for rural land-use can be decided upon it is necessary to examine two other aspects of the overall problem. First, the conflicts which arise over the multiple use of land, and, second, the nature and extent of the costs and bene-fits which might be included, apart from those which are more readily identified. The costs and benefits which each land-use generates could have been dealt with under the respective head-ings above, but it is convenient, bearing in mind that it is agri-culture which is under scrutiny, to consider the additional costs and benefits of the industry in one place. This is done in Section 3 below, following the examination of multiple land-use.


2  MULTIPLE LAND-USES

The economic basis of analysis is that relating to joint and com-plementary products, which form the very core of much of the work on agriculture production economics, reference to which was made in the section on supply in Chapter 1. In the context of rural land-use, where the characteristics of the environment are important as a determinant of recreational demand and where conservation is under consideration, the objective function relates to society at large not to the farmer, so needs to be reformulated. Bunce [116] makes the point in relation to soil conservation, and, in a rather different context of food production, so does Crutchfield [118]. Barnett and Morse [114], Boulding [115], Ciriacy Wantrup [117], Hotelling [119] and Kneese *et al.* [120] are concerned with much wider issues which involve the quality of the environment in addition to the conservation of resources. Barnett and Morse, Hotelling and Ciriacy Wantrup take the relatively optimistic and strictly economic view, but Boulding and Kneese are more pessimistic about the mechanisms in society which the optimists argue should achieve conservation of resources. J. V. Krutilla (ed.) *Natural Environments: Studies in Theoretical and Applied Analysis* (Johns Hopkins University Press, 1973), joins forces with the pessimists. He sees a threat to areas of unique scenic value in present trends in land-use. However, at a theoretical level he sees no difficulty in redefining the objective function, provided that the relative importance of the different land-uses has been established or a decision made to weight the function in favour of the highest valued use. Fisher, Krutilla and Cicchetti (Krutilla (ed.) *Natural Environments*) adopt the idea of highest value in developing an approach first mooted by Krutilla [121] on conservation, and rightly point out that conceptual problems can complicate analysis because technical change has reduced the costs of supply of natural resources so that their scarcity is not apparent. As a result decisions to exploit resources can be irreversible; for example, the disappearance or despoliation of the natural environment. In choosing alternatives a function can be selected which maximises the present value of net social returns also including variables which measure the cost of transforming natural resources. To measure the effect of different assumptions about the degree of transformation and conservation (Fisher, Krutilla and Cicchetti use the word 'preservation') a sensitivity analysis could be conducted. While the difficulties at a theoretical level should not be minimised the empirical problems are much more formidable. This is because information on the compatibility of different land-uses is not forthcoming from a common evaluation datum, notwithstanding the problem of establishing the physical capacity of land. For example, the appeal of an area of outstanding beauty may be enhanced or reduced by encroachment of, say, forestry; it may also be susceptible to increased soil erosion. Recreation is probably the most complex type of use to incorporate as it takes many forms and demand for it includes perception of site capacity by the consumer as well as the physical capacity from a supply point of view. For example, how much does access to farm land depend on a feeling of remoteness and at what level of use does recreation destroy the ability of farmers to grow crops? Another example of conflict occurs in relation to the design and construction of reservoirs. The primary object is to supply water, but the question may be posed: to what extent should water-supply authorities adapt the resource to cater for water recreation? The literature on the demand for and supply of recreation indicates clearly the measurement problems faced, particularly in the case of non-priced resources.

The government report on multiple use of land and the review studies already mentioned illustrate the somewhat intuitive approach to land-use. With the advent of the Sports Council and the Countryside Commission there is some evidence that research will increase and be better co-ordinated, but the economist is still noticeably absent from the ranks of those concerned about the effects of agriculture on land-use.

## 3 BENEFITS AND COSTS OF AGRICULTURAL LAND-USE

The measurement of the benefits and costs of agricultural use of land are thought by many to constitute that part of cost–benefit analysis related to intangibles. While this is true of some aspects it is clear that there are direct benefits and costs which have not been correctly identified and in some instances not identified at all. This applies very much to costs, and as a consequence this section appears to be weighted towards their discussion.

## Benefits

The financial benefits of agriculture have been extensively studied and were noted in the chapters on policy. The inclusion of the social benefits ought to incorporate those accruing to farmers and workers and rural communities by maintaining the industry, as well as those to society at large, such as the contribution agriculture makes to the natural environment in terms of landscape, or the amenity value of the countryside. The more direct social benefits have been explored by rural sociologists, very often on the premise that it is more destructive to rural life and results in greater social costs, to force people out of farming than to support agriculture to keep them in. Ruth Gasson ('The Influence of Urbanisation on Farm Ownership and Practice: Some Aspects of the Effects of London on Farms and Farm People in Kent and Sussex', *Studies in Rural Land Use*, no. 7 (Wye, 1966) has touched on the question of who owns farms and for what purpose, suggesting that many non-farmers buy small farms for the amenity value to themselves and therefore make little contribution to maintaining the rural social structure. Yet there is evidence from rural studies in England, Wales and Scotland that depopulation threatens to destroy rural communities and the rural economy (J. Ashton and W. H. Long (eds), The *Remoter Rural Areas of Britain: An Agricultural Adjustment Unit Symposium* (University of Newcastle; Oliver & Boyd, 1972)). How far policies granting hill-farm subsidies have offset the economic pressures bringing depopulation about is difficult to establish. In terms of agriculture's contribution to the amenity value of land the popular view is that it is responsible for the making of the landscape and that the land should be farmed to prevent dereliction which would detract from visual amenity. This is a point of issue, since modern farming methods have been criticised for destroying the landscape and agricultural policy is said to reinforce this. Attitudes to the landscape can be said to be subjective and therefore not susceptible to evaluation, but geographers and planners have made attempts to classify and rank it so that quantification may be a possibility. K. D. Fines ('Landscape Evaluation: A Research Project in East Sussex', *Regional Studies*, vol 2, no. 1, 1968) has developed a method of appraisal which has certainly suffered the charge of subjectivity. E. C. Penning-Rowsell and D. I. Hardy ('Landscape Evaluation and Planning Policy: A Comparative Study in the Wye Valley Area of Outstanding Beauty', *Regional Studies*, vol. 7, no. 2, 1973) have reviewed later studies and tried to move analysis towards a more objective method.

A point worth noting here is that the Common Agriculural Policy (C.A.P.) of the E.E.C. may introduce new pressures on farming with implications for the landscape. Common Agricultural policies make grants for farms of a much smaller size than did those which formerly applied in the United Kingdom. Thus, whereas there was a tendency for policy in the United Kingdom to encourage the formation of larger farm units which would eventually lead to extensive changes in the character of both the lowland and upland landscapes, the C.A.P. is likely to slow down or even curtail the rate of structural change, thereby perpetuating the present farm appearance in hill areas.

The aspects of possible social benefits given are illustrative of the kind of studies which so far have been largely conducted outside the economic appraisals of agriculture; there is now a need to bring these within a kind of cost–benefit framework. This prescription applies equally to the costs of agriculture which are often not identified. Indeed, some financial costs of an indirect nature have been omitted in appraisals done within a purely agricultural context quite apart from social costs.

## Costs

One of the most ill-considered areas of study in agriculture has been the calculation of the cost of subsidies. McCrone [83] was one of the first to highlight the hidden subsidies, that is to say social costs which should be added to the exchequer costs, such as those which result from the operation of the marketing boards in their pricing policies and the imposition of import controls or levies. Of a more subtle influence are those which impose costs on agriculture itself. Bowers ('Efficiency in Agriculture', in *Agriculture* (1972), p. 106), has outlined the social costs of one form of agricultural pollution by referring to the discharge of effluent into the waterway system, but he overlooked the direct cost to the industry in the form of a lost benefit of waste which could be recycled. B. Hodgetts ('Animal Waste in the U.S.A.',

*Agriculture*, vol. 79, no. 3, Mar 1972) and J. M. Oliphant ('Dried Waste and Intensive Beef', *Agriculture*, vol. 79, no. 12, Dec 1972) have estimated that the nutrient content of manure is such that when processed for animal feed as much as 20 per cent of it is reclaimable. Another internal cost to agriculture is the effect on the soil structure of the use of modern machinery and continuous arable cropping, both of which have been reinforced by the policy measures. Fears grew after a very wet season in 1968–9 which resulted in an inquiry and report on farming methods.[1] The conclusions were that soil structure had deteriorated, there was a lack of attention to drainage and that diseases and pests were more difficult to control. There was also some evidence that yields had fallen as the result of intensive monoculture. The problems encountered in the United States are well known through the work of the Tennessee Valley Authority. The contributions of Bunce [116], Ciriacy Wantrup [117] and Hotelling [119], to the economics of conservation are important in this context. If a full cost–benefit study were being made of policy it is possible that what is referred to here as an internal cost to agriculture could be construed as a social cost if viewed from society's point of view, especially if it necessitated payment of higher subsidies to maintain an agreed level of agricultural income.

In terms of what is normally accepted as a social cost there is a growing list of studies which pinpoint both government policy and agricultural activity as perpetrators. There is prima facie strong evidence linking the effect on farm practice – and, consequently, the environment – of capital grants, fertiliser subsidies and production grants. Pollution through the leaching of fertilisers and pesticides through the soil into water-supply and natural drainage systems and the effects of residual chemicals on wild life have now been extensively studied; K. Mellanby's[2] is an example of work done in this field. The effect on the landscape of farm building, which is not subject to planning controls, has been assessed by J. Clayton ('Farm Buildings in a Planned

[1] Report of the Agricultural Advisory Council on Soil Structure and Soil Fertility, *Modern Farming and the Soil* (The Strutt Report) (H.M.S.O., 1970).

[2] *Pesticides and Pollution* (Collins, 1967).

Environment' (unpublished University of London Ph.D. thesis, 1971)) and mention has already been made of planners and geographers who have observed the despoliation of the landscape by farming. Conservationists have produced a flood of information on the impact on the ecological balance of the removal of hedges and trees, the ploughing up of natural habitats and afforestation. A conference at Silsoe was an important milestone in the conflict between conservationists and farmers, for it highlighted their essential differences. The report of this conference can be found in D. Barber (ed.), *Farming and Wildlife: A Study in Compromise* (Royal Society for the Protection of Birds, 1970). Finally, the incompatibilities between farming and recreation, to which some reference has already been made, have been pointed out by the official bodies, such as the Countryside Commission, the National Trust and local authorities, and those studying the interrelationship between recreation and other land-uses. The nature of the conflict, apart from difficulties of access, really embraces all the social costs specified in this section as the degree of pollution, visual intrusion, despoliation and destruction of the environment all affect the amenity value of rural land in the context of recreation.

Much of the conflict between agriculture and other land-uses and the existence of the serious social costs which agriculture imposes on society can undoubtedly be attributed to decisions to expand agriculture after the Second World War. Bowers ('Efficiency in Agriculture') quite rightly connects agricultural policy with these costs, but he is apt to overstate his case by underrating the pressure of economic forces which would have radically altered farming methods anyway. In any event it is almost impossible to establish the extent to which policy is responsible except in isolated cases. A more disturbing aspect of policy-induced methods is that they reinforce the economic pressures against which regulations or advisory services emanating from the Minstry of Agriculture, Fisheries and Food and legislation, such as the Countryside Act, seem virtually powerless and anachronistic. It is also clearly illogical that farmers should be given grants to plough up hill pastures or root out hedges at the same time as bodies such as the Nature Conservancy or the Countryside Commission are set up with the purpose of protecting wild

81

life and conserving the amenity value of the countryside. It is certainly true that in the past the situation which has now occurred was not foreseen and, furthermore, it could be argued that a methodological framework in which agriculture could be fitted, alongside consideration of other land-uses, had not been developed. Therefore, in retrospect, agricultural policy decisions appear to have been pragmatic and isolated from other land-use policy. At present there are continued misgivings about the usefulness of cost–benefit analysis in relation to land-use decisions, especially where there are difficulties of measurement. It follows that many of the social costs of agriculture specified above might not be included in an appraisal, even though identified. This is not the place to discuss in detail the problems of measuring intangibles,[1] but the Fisher, Krutilla and Cicchetti (Krutilla (ed.), *Natural Environments*) approach of specifying a function which takes account of the costs of each land-use activity on a weighting basis rather than in purely monetary terms could prove fruitful. Although agriculture's contribution to G.N.P. is only 3 per cent, it is one of the largest single industries and uses 80 per cent of the total land area in the United Kingdom. It would therefore seem appropriate that the impact of changes in its activity might necessitate something approaching a general equilibrium analysis. Such a notion is sufficient to indicate the magnitude of the task in undertaking a meaningful appraisal of the industry.

A disclaimer was made at the beginning of this chapter that the examination of land-use would not extend beyond the United Kingdom. However, it should be apparent that the United States has contributed most to the literature on land-use despite, in comparison with European countries, the much lower pressure on land-use. This reflects, perhaps, a greater awareness in that country of some acute problems raised by rapid economic growth. It is clear that European countries face very much the same problems, and therefore, although the sources and examples are drawn almost entirely from the United Kingdom or the United States, very much the same picture would result if the situation in Europe were examined.

[1] See Pearce, *Cost-Benefit Analysis* (Macmillan, 1971).

82

# 5 Conclusions

An attempt has been made in this review to trace the influence of agriculture on the economies of industrial nations and the development of economic analysis related to the industry. Apart from some obvious gaps, such as the examination of the international trade in food products and the significance of agricultural surpluses to growth, the approach has been to accent the theme that certain areas of agricultural activity, which are important determinants of the pattern of rural land-use, have been neglected. It is hoped that a fair indication has been given of where economists have failed to make an impact and why. Much space has been devoted to government activity and the implications of its policy devices because of the effect these have on the existing pressures on the use of rural land and because they dictate the direction in which research should proceed. It is apparent that outside the studies of a specific nature related to farm management a new breed of economists is required, because agricultural economists have hardly begun to comprehend the ramifications of wider issues on their own studies. Rural environment economics or rural land economics would adequately describe their sphere of interest, and, at the present state of knowledge, much of their work would be conducted within a kind of cost–benefit analysis framework. The topics of immediate concern would certainly include :

(*a*) more detailed appraisals of the economic costs of agricultural policy, both domestic and foreign;

(*b*) the study of human resources in agriculture on a multi-disciplinary basis;

(*c*) the empirical investigation of the different forms of rural land-use and

(*d*) the development of methodologies for the appraisal of land-use in conjunction with other disciplines such as social psychology, sociology, planning and law.

# Bibliography

The bibliography is divided into two sections; Section A lists a selection of elementary and general references on economics and agriculture, and Section B contains references, listed alphabetically by author, under the main subject areas covered in the text.

SECTION A

[1a] E. O. Heady, *Economics of Agricultural Production and Resource Use* (Prentice-Hall, 1952).
[2a] A. Martin, *Economics and Agriculture* (Routledge & Kegan Paul, 1958).
[3a] D. Metcalf, *The Economics of Agriculture* (Penguin, 1969).
[4a] T. W. Schultz, *Economic Organisation of Agriculture* (McGraw-Hill, 1953).
[5a] R. H. Tuck, *An Introduction to the Principles of Agricultural Economics* (Longmans, 1961).


SECTION B

CAPITAL AND LAND

[1] M. Bandini *et al.*, *Agriculture and Economic Growth* (O.E.C.D., 1965).
[2] C. J. Black, 'Capital Deployment on Farms in Theory and Practice', *Farm Economist*, vol. 10, no. 12; vol. 11, no. 1 (1965–6).
[3] S. N. Cheung, *The Theory of Share Tenancy* (University of Chicago Press, 1969).
[4] C. Clark, 'The Value of Agricultural Land', *Journal of Agricultural Economics*, vol. 20, no. 1 (1969).
[5] K. D. Cocks, 'Discounted Cash Flow and Agricultural Investment', *Journal of Agricultural Economics*, vol. 16, no. 4 (1965).
[6] G. E. Dalton, 'Simulation Models for the Specification of Farm Investment Plans', *Journal of Agricultural Economics*, vol. 22, no. 2 (1971).

[7] R. N. Dixey and A. H. Maunder, 'Planning Again: A Study of Farm Size and Layout', *Farm Economist*, vol. 9, no. 6 (1959).

[8] Z. Griliches, 'The Sources of Measured Productivity Growth: U.S. Agriculture, 1940–60', *Journal of Political Economy*, vol. 21, no. 4 (1963).

[9] E. O. Heady, G. L. Johnson and L. S. Hardin, *Resource Productivity, Returns to Scale and Farm Size* (Iowa State University Press, 1956).

[10] E. O. Heady, 'Optimal Size of Farms Under Varying Tenure Forms', *American Journal of Agricultural Economics*, vol. 53, no. 1 (1971).

[11] R. A. Hoffman and E. O. Heady, *Production-Income and Resource Changes, Farm Consolidation* (Iowa Research Bulletin 502, 1962).

[12] A. H. Maunder, 'Fixed Equipment in Agriculture', *Farm Economist*, vol. 10, no. 2 (1969).

[13] Ministry of Agriculture, Fisheries and Food (M.A.F.F.), 'Productivity Measurement in Agriculture', *Economic Trends*, no. 189 (July 1969).

[14] A. A. Montgomery and J. R. Tarbet, 'Land Returns and Farm Real Estate Values', *Agricultural Economics Research*, vol. 20, no. 1 (1968).

[15] G. H. Peters, 'Recent Trends in Farm Real Estate Values in England and Wales', *Farm Economist*, vol. 11, no. 2 (1966).

[16] G. H. Peters, 'Capital and Labour in British Agriculture', *Farm Economist*, vol. 11, no. 2 (1967).

[17] S. A. Robson, 'Agriculture and Economic Growth', *Journal of Agricultural Economics*, vol. 21, no. 2 (1970).

[18] R. Schickele, 'Effect of Tenure Systems on Agricultural Efficiency', *Journal of Farm Economics*, vol. 23 (1941).

[19] G. Sharp and C. W. Capstick, 'The Place of Agriculture in the National Economy', *Journal of Agricultural Economics*, vol. 17, no. 1 (1966).

[20] D. Warriner, *Land Reform in Principle and Practice* (Oxford, 1969).

## DEMAND ANALYSIS

[21] G. Ackley, *Macroeconomics* (Collier–Macmillan, 1966).

[22] R. G. D. Allen and A. L. Bowley, *Family Expenditure* (P. S. King & Son, 1935).

[23] R. J. Ball, J. R. Eaton and M. A. Henderson, 'The Demand for Eggs in Shell in the United Kingdom', *Journal of Agricultural Economics*, vol. 18, no. 2 (1967).

[24] M. C. Burk, *Consumption Economics: A Multidisciplinary Approach* (Wiley, 1968).

[25] D. Engel, *Die Productions und Consumptionverhaltnisse des Königreichs Sachsen*, reprinted 1895 in *Bulletin de l'Institut International de Statistique*, vol. 9 (1857).

[26] Food and Agricultural Organisation (F.A.O.), *Food Consumption Statistics, 1961–8* (Paris, 1970).

[27] Z. A. Hassan, R. M. Finley and S. R. Johnson, 'The Demand for Food in the United States', *Applied Economics*, vol. 5, no. 4 (Dec 1973).

[28] H.M.S.O., *Family Expenditure Survey* (Annual).

[29] H. S. Houthakker, 'An International Comparison of Household Expenditure Patterns, Commemorating the Centenary of Engel's Law', *Econometrica*, vol. 25, no. 4 (1957).

[30] G. Katona, *Psychological Analysis of Economic Behaviour* (McGraw-Hill, 1951).

[31] G. M. Kuznets, 'Measurement of Market Demand with Particular Reference to Consumer Demand for Food', *Journal of Farm Economics*, vol. 35, no. 5 (1953).

[32] C. E. V. Leser, 'Forms of Engel Functions', *Econometrica*, vol. 31, no. 4 (1963).

[33] O.E.C.D., *Agricultural Projections for 1975–1985, Production and Consumption of Major Foodstuffs* (1968).

[34] S. J. Prais and H. S. Houthakker, *The Analysis of Family Budgets* (Cambridge University Press, 1955).

[35] A. S. Rojko, 'Time Series Analysis in Measurement of Demand', *Agricultural Economics Research*, vol. 13, no. 2 (1961).

[36] J. M. Slater, 'Regional Consumer Expenditure Studies Using National Food Survey Data', *Journal of Agricultural Economics*, vol. 20, no. 2 (1969).

[37] United States Department of Agriculture (U.S.D.A.) Economic Research Service, *Food Consumption, Prices Expenditures*, Agricultural Economics Report No. 138 (July and supplement for 1968, Washington, 1968).

[38] R. E. Williams, 'The Problem of the size of the Milk Industry in the U.K.', *Journal of Agricultural Economics*, vol. 22, no. 1 (1971).

[39] J. R. Bellerby, *Agriculture and Industry: Relative Income* (Macmillan, 1956).

[40] M. Black, 'Agricultural Labour in an Expanding Economy', *Journal of Agricultural Economics*, vol. 24, no. 1 (1968).

[41] R. Gasson, 'Use of Sociology in Agricultural Economics', *Journal of Agricultural Economics*, vol. 22, no. 1 (1971).

[42] H. D. Guither, 'Factors Influencing Farm Operators Decisions to Leave Farming', *Journal of Farm Economics*, vol. 45, no. 3 (1963).

[43] D. Hathaway and B. Perkins, 'Farm Labour Mobility, Migration and Income Distribution', *American Journal of Agricultural Economics*, vol. 50, no. 2 (1968).

[44] G. L. Johnson, 'The Labour Utilisation Problems in European and American Agriculture', *Journal of Agricultural Economics*, vol. 14, no. 1 (1960).

[45] J. W. McGuire, *Theories of Business Behaviour* (Prentice-Hall, 1964).

[46] J. G. Maddox, 'Historical Review of the Nation's Efforts to Cope with Rural Poverty', *American Journal of Agricultural Economics*, vol. 50, no. 4 (1968).

[47] D. Metcalf, 'Determinants of the Earnings Gap in Agriculture in England and Wales, 1948–63', *Farm Economist*, vol. 11, no. 2 (1966).

[48] H. Newby, 'The Low Earnings of Agricultural Workers – A Sociological Approach', *Journal of Agricultural Economics*, vol. 23, no. 1 (1972).

[49] H. A. Simon, 'Theories of Decision-Making in Economics and Behavioural Science', *American Economic Review*, vol. 49, no. 3 (1959).

[50] T. T. Stout and V. W. Rattan, 'Regional Differences in Factor Shares in American Agriculture, 1925–1957', *Journal of Farm Economics*, vol, 42, no. 1 (1960).

[51] D. C. Thorns, 'The Influence of Social Change on the Farmer', *Farm Economist*, vol. 11, no. 8 (1968).

[52] D. S. Thornton, 'The Study of Decision-Making and its Relevance to the Study of Farm Management', *Farm Economist*, vol. 10, nos. 1 & 2 (1962).

MARKETING

[53] G. R. Allen, 'Marketing of Fatstock and Carcase Meat', *Farm Economist*, vol. 10, no. 4 (1963).

[54] G. R. Allen, 'An Appraisal of Contract Farming', *Journal of Agricultural Economics*, vol. 23, no. 2 (1972).

[55] R. L. Clodius and W. F. Mueller, 'Market Structure Analysis as an Orientation for Research in Agricultural Economics', *Journal of Farm Economics*, vol. 43, no. 3 (1961).

[56] R. L. Cohen, 'Further Reflections on Agricultural Marketing', *Journal of Agricultural Economics*, vol. 14, no. 4 (1961).

[57] J. L. Davies, 'Reflections on the Marketing of Own Farm Produce', *Journal of Agricultural Economics*, vol. 14, no. 2 (1960).

[58] P. L. Farris (ed.), *Market Structure Research* (Iowa State University Press, 1964).

[59] M. M. Guter and E. M. Low, 'The British Egg Marketing Board, 1957–71 – A Reassessment', *Journal of Agricultural Economics*, vol. 22, no. 3 (1971).

[60] P. G. Helmberger, 'Co-operative Enterprise as a Structural Dimension of Farm Markets', *Journal of Farm Economics*, vol. 46, no. 3 (1964).

[61] G. Houston, 'Meat Marketing Margins in Britain', *Journal of Agricultural Economics*, vol. 15, no. 1 (1962).

[62] R. L. Kohls, *The Marketing of Agricultural Products* (Macmillan, 1965).

[63] J. R. Moore and R. G. Walsh, *Market Structure of the Agricultural Industry* (Iowa State University Press, 1966).

[64] A. B. Paul, 'Integration in Food and Agricultural Industries', *American Economic Review*, vol. 15, no. 3 (1963).

[65] E. P. Roy, 'Effective Competition and Changing Patterns in Marketing Broiler Chickens', *Journal of Farm Economics*, vol. 48, no. 3 (1966).

[66] G. S. Shepherd, *Marketing Agricultural Products*, 4th ed. (Iowa State University Press, 1962).

[67] T. K. Warley, 'The Future Role of Marketing Organisations', *Journal of Agricultural Economics*, vol. 15, no. 4 (1963).

[68] T. K. Warley (ed.), *Agricultural Producers and their Markets* (Oxford, 1967).

[69] D. Wood, 'Welfare Aspects of Pricing Policies for Agricultural Commodities', *Farm Economist*, vol. 10, no. 9 (1965).

[70] G. R. Allen, *Agricultural Marketing Policies* (Blackwell, 1959).

[71] M. Butterwick and E. Neville-Rolfe, 'Structural Reform in French Agriculture: The Work of the S.A.F.E.R.S.', *Journal of Agricultural Economics*, vol. 16, no. 4 (1965).

[72] M. Butterwick and E. Neville-Rolfe, *Agricultural Marketing and the E.E.C.* (Hutchinson, 1970).

[73] F. Deakin, *Agriculture and the E.E.C.* (Fabian Pamphlet, 1971).

[74] G. W. Dean and H. O. Carter, 'Some Effects of Income Taxes on Large Scale Agriculture', *Journal of Farm Economics*, vol. 44, no. 3 (1962).

[75] Economic Development Council for the Agricultural Industry (E.D.C.), *Agriculture's Import-Saving Role* (H.M.S.O., 1968).

[76] A. F. Evans, 'Impact of Taxation on Agriculture', *Journal of Agricultural Economics*, vol. 20, no. 2 (1969).

[77] J. K. Galbraith, 'Economic Preconceptions and the Farm Policy', *American Economic Review*, vol. 44, no. 1 (1954).

[78] G. Hallett, *The Economics of Agricultural Policy* (Blackwell, 1968).

[79] D. E. Hathaway, *Government and Agriculture* (Macmillan, 1963).

[80] H.M.S.O., *The Development of Agriculture*, Cmnd 2738 (Aug 1965).

[81] Iowa State University: Center for Agricultural and Economic Development, *Food, Goals, Future Structural Changes and Agricultural Policy: A National Basebook* (Iowa State University Press, 1969).

[82] T. Josling, 'A Formal Approach to Agricultural Policy', *Journal of Agricultural Economics*, vol. 20, no. 2 (1969).

[83] G. McCrone, *The Economics of Subsidising Agriculture* (Allen & Unwin, 1962).

[84] A. M. M. McFarquhar and M. C. Evans, 'Projection Models for United Kingdom Food and Agriculture', *Journal of Agricultural Economics*, vol. 22, no. 3 (1971).

[85] J. Marsh and C. Ritson, *Agricultural Policy and the Common Market* (Chatham House [P.E.P.], 1971).

[86] E. F. Nash, *Agricultural Policy in Britain* (University of Wales, 1963).

[87] Natural Resources (Technical Committee), *Scale of Enterprise in Farming* (H.M.S.O., 1961).

[88] O.E.C.D. Agricultural Policy Reports, *Interrelationship Between Income and Supply Problems in Agriculture* (1965).

[89] O.E.C.D. Agricultural Policy Reports, *Structural Reform Measures in Agriculture* (1972).

[90] D. Paarlberg, *American Farm Policy* (Wiley, 1964).

[91] U. Papi and C. Nunn, *Economic Problems of Agriculture in Developed Countries*, Proceedings of a Conference held by the International Economic Association (Macmillan, 1969).

[92] W. D. Rasmussen and G. L. Baker, 'A Short History of Price Support and Adjustment Legislation and Programs for Agriculture, 1933–65', *Agricultural Economics Research*, vol. 18, no. 3 (1966).

[93] R. C. Rickard, 'Structural Policies for Agriculture, in the E.E.C.', *Journal of Agricultural Economics*, vol. 21, no. 3 (1970).

[94] C. Ritson, 'The Use of Home Resources to Save Imports: A New Look', *Journal of Agricultural Economics*, vol. 21, no. 1 (1970).

[95] E. A. G. Robinson, 'The Future of British Imports', *Three Banks Review* (June 1958).

[96] R. Schickele, *Agricultural Policy* (University of Nebraska Press, 1954).

[97] G. S. Shepherd, *Farm Policy: New Directions* (Iowa State University Press, 1964).

[98] J. Southgate, *Agricultural Trade and the E.E.C.* (Institute of Economic Affairs, London, 1970).

[99] V. F. Stewart, 'The Agricultural Problems in Estate Duty Taxation', *Farm Economist*, vol. 10, no. 10 (1965).

[100] M. Tracy, *Agriculture in Western Europe* (Cape, 1964).

[101] H. R. Wagstaff, 'The Economic Surplus of Agriculture in the United Kingdom', *Journal of Agricultural Economics*, vol. 23, no. 3 (1972).

# RISK AND UNCERTAINTY

[102] R. C. Agrawal and E. O. Heady, 'Applications of Game Theory Models in Agriculture', *Journal of Agricultural Economics*, vol. 19, no. 2 (1968).

[103] J. L. Dillon, 'Applications of Game Theory in Agricultural Economics: Review and Requiem', *Australian Journal of Agricultural Economics*, vol. 6 (1962).

[104] J. Dixon, 'Uncertainty and Information in Agriculture', *Farm Economist*, vol. 11, no. 4 (1967).

[105] J. P. Doll, 'An Analytical Technique for Estimating Weather Indices from Meteorological Measurements', *Journal of Farm Economics*, vol. 49, no. 1 (1967).

[106] P. B. R. Hazell, 'Game Theory: Extension of its Application to Farm Planning under Uncertainty', *Journal of Agricultural Economics*, vol. 21, no. 2 (1970).

[107] S. R. Johnson, 'A Re-examination of Farm Diversification Problems', *Journal of Farm Economics*, vol. 49, no. 3 (1967).

[108] H. M. Markowitz, *Portfolio Selection*, Cowles Foundation (Wiley, 1959).

[109] L. H. Shaw, 'The Effects of Weather on Agricultural Output: A Look at Methodology', *Journal of Farm Economics*, vol. 46, no. 1 (1964).

## RURAL LAND-USE

*General*

[110] K. Openshaw, 'Note: A Critical Look at Rural Land Use Assessment', *Journal of Agricultural Economics*, vol. 19, no. 3 (1968).

[111] G. H. Peters, 'Land-use Studies in Britain: A Review', *Journal of Agricultural Economics*, vol. 21, no. 2 (1970).

[112] J. T. Ward, 'The Siting of Urban Development in Agricultural Land', *Journal of Agricultural Economics*, vol. 12, no. 4 (Dec 1957).

[113] G. P. Wibberley, *Agriculture and Economic Growth* (Joseph, 1959).

*Conservation*

[114] H. J. Barnett and C. Morse, *Scarcity and Growth: the Economics of Natural Resource Availability* (Johns Hopkins Press, 1963).

[115] R. Boulding, 'The Economics of the Coming Spaceship Earth', in *Environmental Quality in a Growing Economy*, Essays from the 1966 RFF Forum, ed. H. Jarrett (Johns Hopkins Press, 1966)·

[116] A. C. Bunce, *Economics of Soil Conservation* (Iowa State University Press, 1945).

[117] S. V. Ciriacy Wantrup, *Resource Conservation* (University of California, 1952).

[118] J. A. Crutchfield, 'Valuation of Fisheries Resources', *Land Economics*, vol. 38, no. 2 (May 1962).

[119] H. Hotelling, 'The Economics of Exhaustible Resources', *Journal of Political Economy*, vol. 39 (1931).

[120] A. V. Kneese *et al.*, *Economics and the Environment: A Materials Balance Approach. Resources for the Future* (Johns Hopkins Press, 1970).

[121] J. V. Krutilla, 'Conservation Reconsidered', *American Economic Review*, vol. 57, no. 4 (1967).

*Forestry*

[122] Department of Education and Science (D.E.S.), *Report of the Land Use Study Group – Forestry Agriculture and the Multiple Use of Rural Land* (H.M.S.O., 1966).

[123] S. F. Hampson, 'Highland Forestry: An Evaluation', *Journal of Agricultural Economics*, vol. 23, no. 1 (1970).

[124] G. James, 'Economic Appraisal of the Use of Hills and Uplands for Forestry and Agriculture Respectively', *Farm Economist*, vol. 10, no. 12 (1965).

[125] R. Lorraine-Smith, *The Economy of the Private Woodland in Great Britain* (University of Oxford, 1969).

[126] Ministry of Agriculture, Fisheries and Food (M.A.F.F.), *Forest Policy* (H.M.S.O., 1972).

[127] Natural Resources (Technical Committee), *Forestry, Agricultural and Marginal Land* (H.M.S.O., 1957).

[128] K. R. Walker, 'The Forestry Commission and the Use of Hill Land', *Scottish Journal of Political Economy*, vol. 7, no. 1 (1960).

*Recreation*

[129] T. L. Burton and P. A. Noad, *Recreation Research Method: A Review of Recent Studies*, Occasional Paper No. 3, Centre for Urban and Regional Studies, University of Birmingham (1968).

[130] M. Clawson, *Methods of Measuring the Demand for and Value of Outdoor Recreation: Resources for the Future*, Reprint no. 10 (Johns Hopkins Press, 1959).

[131] M. Clawson and J. L. Knetsch, *The Economics of Outdoor Recreation* (Johns Hopkins Press, 1966).

[132] Countryside Commission, *The Demand for Outdoor Recreation in the Countryside*, Report of Seminar (Jan 1970).

[133] Countryside Commission, *Recreation Cost–Benefit Analysis*, Report of Seminar (Feb 1971).
[134] C. B. Keenleyside, *Farming, Landscape and Recreation* (Countryside Commission, 1971).
[135] Outdoor Recreation Resources Review Commission, *Outdoor Recreation for America*, Series of Papers on Recreation (Washington, 1962).
[136] A. Phillips and M. Roberts, 'The Recreation and Amenity Value of the Countryside', *Journal of Agricultural Economics*, vol. 24, no. 1 (Jan 1973).


*Water*

[137] O. Eckstein, *Water Resource Development* (Harvard, 1958).
[138] A. V. Kneese and S. C. Smith, *Water Research, Resources for the Future* (Johns Hopkins Press, 1966).

## SUPPLY ANALYSIS

[139] K. Cowling, D. Metcalf and A. J. Rayner, *Resource Structure of Agriculture: An Economic Analysis* (Pergamon, 1970).
[140] Z. Griliches, 'Demand for Fertilizer, an Economic Interpretation of a Technical Change', *Journal of Farm Economics*, vol. 40, no. 3 (1958).
[141] Z. Griliches, 'Estimates of the Aggregate United States Farm Supply Function', *Journal of Farm Economics*, vol. 42, no. 2 (1960).
[142] E. O. Heady and J. L. Dillon, *Agricultural Production Functions* (Iowa State University Press, 1960).
[143] E. O. Heady and L. G. Tweeten, *Resource Demand and the Structure of the Agricultural Industry* (Iowa State University Press, 1963).
[144] D. F. Heathfield, *Production Functions* (Macmillan, 1971).
[145] R. Howard, *Dynamic Programming and Markov Chain Processes* (Cambridge, Mass.: Harvard University Press, 1960).
[146] G. T. Jones, 'The Response of the Supply of Agricultural Products in the U.K. to Price', *Farm Economist*, vol. 9, no. 12 (1961); vol. 10, no. 1 (1962).
[147] M. Nerlove, 'Distributed Lags and Estimation of Long-Run Supply and Demand Elasticities: Theoretical Considerations', *Journal of Farm Economics*, vol. 40, no. 2 (1958).

[148] M. Nerlove, *The Dynamics of Supply: Estimation of Farmers' Response to Price* (Johns Hopkins Press, 1958).

[149] A. J. Rayner and K. Cowling, 'Demand for Farm Tractors in the United States and the United Kingdom', *American Journal of Agricultural Economics*, vol. 50, no. 4 (1968).

[150] G. E. Schuh, 'An Econometric Investigation of the Market for Hired Labour in Agriculture', *Journal of Farm Economics*, vol. 44, no. 2 (1962).

*Technical change and diffusion of innovations*

[151] L. A. Brown, *Diffusion Processes and Location: Conceptual Framework*, Regional Science Research Institute, Bibliography Series no. 4 (Philadelphia, 1968).

[152] Z. Griliches, 'Hybrid Corn: An Exploration in the Economics of Technical Change', *Econometrica*, vol. 25, no. 4 (1957).

[153] G. E. Jones, 'The Diffusion of Agricultural Innovations', *Journal of Agricultural Economics*, vol. 15, no. 3 (1963).

[154] G. E. Jones, 'The Adoption and Diffusion of Agricultural Practices', *World Agricultural Economics and Rural Sociology Abstracts*, reprint of review article (Commonwealth Agricultural Bureaux, 1967).

[155] E. M. Rogers, 'Categorizing the Adopters of Agricultural Practices', *Rural Sociology*, vol. 23, no. 4 (1958).

[156] H. T. E. Smith, 'Some Notes on the Adoption of Farm Practices', *Farm Economist*, vol. 10, nos. 8 and 9 (1964/5).

[157] R. M. Solow, 'Investment and Technical Progress', in *Mathematical Methods in the Social Services*, ed. K. J. Arrow (Stanford University Press, 1959).